INSIGHT GUIDES

EXPLORE

D0005541

MIAMI

◉ Walking Eye App

YOUR FREE EBOOK AVAILABLE THROUGH THE WALKING EYE APP

Your guide now includes a free eBook to your chosen destination, for the same great price as before. Simply download the Walking Eye App from the App Store or Google Play to access your free eBook.

HOW THE WALKING EYE APP WORKS

Through the Walking Eye App, you can purchase a range of eBooks and destination content. However, when you buy this book, you can download the corresponding eBook for free. Just see below in the grey panel where to find your free content and then scan the QR code at the bottom of this page.

Destinations: Download essential destination content featuring recommended sights and attractions, restaurants, hotels and an A–Z of practical information, all available for purchase.

Ships: Interested in ship reviews? Find independent reviews of river and ocean ships in this section, all available for purchase.

eBooks: You can download your free accompanying digital version of this guide here. You will also find a whole range of other eBooks, all available for purchase.

Free access to travel-related blog articles about different destinations, updated on a daily basis.

HOW THE EBOOKS WORK

The eBooks are provided in EPUB file format. Please note that you will need an eBook reader installed on your device to open the file. Many devices come with this as standard, but you may still need to install one manually from Google Play.

The eBook content is identical to the content in the printed guide.

HOW TO DOWNLOAD THE WALKING EYE APP

1. Download the Walking Eye App from the App Store or Google Play.
2. Open the app and select the scanning function from the main menu.
3. Scan the QR code on this page – you will then be asked a security question to verify ownership of the book.
4. Once this has been verified, you will see your eBook in the purchased ebook section, where you will be able to download it.

Other destination apps and eBooks are available for purchase separately or are free with the purchase of the Insight Guide book.

CONTENTS

ARCHITECTURE FANS

Miami is renowned for its Art Deco architecture and especially its Art Deco hotels (route 1) which can be enjoyed, inside and out, whether you stay in one or not.

RECOMMENDED ROUTES FOR...

ART LOVERS

Miami's love affair with art is ongoing, with new galleries and regular art walks in places such as North Miami (route 4), South Beach (route 2), and the Wynwood neighborhood (route 5).

BACK TO NATURE

With the Everglades on the doorstep it would be a shame not to see at least a little of them, and one fun way is to do so on two wheels (route 13).

BEACH ENTHUSIASTS

Miami is a city break and beach vacation all in one neat package. Renting a bike to explore South Beach (route 3) and Virginia Key and Key Biscayne (route 11) is a great way to enjoy those beaches.

HISTORY BUFFS

Art Deco isn't the only historical interest Miami has. A simple walk in Coconut Grove (route 12) or the Overtown neighborhood (route 6) reveals plenty of other historic gems.

ISLAND HOPPING

As attractive as Miami is, you should rent a car and get out at least once. Going through the Florida Keys (route 14) is one of the US's greatest driving experiences.

NIGHT OWLS

Miami buzzes day and night but if you love your nightlife you have to head for Little Havana (route 7) which rocks to its own Latin beat.

SHOPPING

Downtown Miami (route 8) is just one of the city's many shopping hubs, and here you can combine it with a walk along the waterfront.

INTRODUCTION

An introduction to Miami's geography, customs and culture, plus illuminating background information on cuisine, history and what to do when you're there.

EXPLORE MIAMI

Renowned for its beaches and perfect winter climate, Miami also offers a wide variety of other attractions. It's noted for its architecture as well as for its lively nightlife, while the natural beauty of the Everglades is right on the doorstep.

Sandwiched between sandy beaches and the swampy Everglades, Miami's diversity helps make it the vibrant city that it is. Its noted Art Deco architecture comes from a boom period when Miami was *the* vacation destination, especially for New Yorkers heading south in search of the sun. That still happens today, and the city attracts numerous snowbirds – people escaping the cold winters of the northern US and Canada. It's also long been a magnet for people heading north from the Caribbean, seeking a better life in the US, notably from Haiti, the Dominican Republic, Jamaica, and Cuba especially. Throw into the mix its appeal as a holiday destination to travelers from all over the world, and you discover that New York isn't the only place in America that can claim to be a melting pot and a city that never sleeps.

GEOGRAPHY AND LAYOUT

The routes in this book cover the different districts and neighborhoods that make up Miami and the area around it. You'll soon get to know the difference between Miami, Miami Beach, South Beach, South Miami, North Miami, Miami Shores, and all the other places that fit into the geographical jigsaw that we know simply as Miami.

The routes start in the east, in Miami Beach (see page 30), located on the mix of natural and man-made islands that are off-shore in the Atlantic Ocean. South Beach (see pages 36 and 39) is simply the southern part of Miami Beach, and from there the routes jump to North Miami (see page 42) and run roughly north-south through the atmospheric neighborhoods of Overtown (see page 50) and Little Havana (see page 54). Virginia Key and Key Biscayne (see page 70) are also off-shore islands, with the extreme south of the city explored in Coconut Grove (see page 74), one of the oldest parts of the city. Finally, on Miami's doorstep are two delightful escapes, one to the Everglades in the west (see page 79), the other to the Florida Keys in the south, one of the most picturesque drives in the US (see page 84).

That sounds like a lot of exploring, and the best way to do it is to combine walking with the excellent and inexpensive public transportation system (see

The high-rises of Downtown Miami and Brickell Key

page 117). If you don't want to bother with bus and rail, taxis are widely available (see page 117). Just be aware that the traffic in Miami can be very heavy at times, and you could spend a lot of time sitting in it. It might not seem an obvious choice, but Miami is a bike-friendly city and renting a bike (see page 117) allows you to explore at your own pace and get fit all the while.

HISTORY

Miami gets its name from the Miami River, which flows from the Everglades through the city and out into Biscayne Bay. The river is connected to Lake Okeechobee by the Miami Canal, the lake's original name being Lake Mayaimi, for the Native American Mayaimi people who lived around it. The Native American people who actually lived in what is now Miami were the Tequestas, who had inhabited this part of the Florida coast since at least 600BC, though they had moved on by the time the first Europeans arrived in the mid-16th century. The Spanish built a mission here, as they vied with the French and the British for control of Florida, though it wasn't till 1870 that a trading post was established, marking the beginnings of Miami.

By 1884 the new settlement's first hotel was built in Coconut Grove, the city's oldest continuously-inhabited neighborhood (see page 74). Miami was then incorporated as a city in 1896, the same year that the Florida East Coast Railway extended its network to reach Miami at the request of local businesswoman and landowner Julia Tuttle, thus making Miami the only major American city to be founded by a woman.

Tuttle's initiative led to the growth of the city as a major transportation hub for the area's developing agricultural industry. Tourists began coming too, spurring on a boom in hotels, theaters, cinemas and other recreational facilities – and Miami soon became known as the Magic City. The 1930s saw the construction of a number of beautiful Art Deco buildings, many of which still stand today (see page 30). In the

Miami Beach

Ocean Drive, at the heart of the Art Deco district of South Beach

1950s, the first wave of Cuban immigrants arrived on the Miami shores, settling mostly in the area now known as Little Havana (see page 54). Since then the city has continued to expand and to attract visitors, notably cruise passengers, confirming its status as number-one busiest cruise ports in the world.

CLIMATE

Miami has a subtropical monsoon climate, meaning it has a hot and humid rainy season that runs from about May to the middle of October. This is also hurricane season, so not the best time to plan a visit, although hurricanes aren't common and the rain that does

DON'T LEAVE MIAMI WITHOUT...

Dining in Little Havana. Get a taste of Cuba without leaving the US, and throw in some Cuban music too while you're at it. See page 58.

Learning about Art Deco. Admire the city's iconic Art Deco buildings dating from the 1930s and 40s, especially in South Beach, by following our Art Deco route. See page 30.

Going to the Everglades. Whether you go under your own steam by bike (see page 79) or join an organised excursion, take the chance to see the US's third-largest national park and the country's biggest tropical wilderness.

Biking It. Miami is a great metropolis, with a vast amount of traffic, but local people know that one of the best ways of getting about is on two wheels, whether for leisure or simply to get from A to B. See pages 24 and 39.

Taking a beach day. Of course you may plan to spend every day on the beach, but if you're in Miami for the culture or the activities, you should still try to make time to chill out for a few hours on the beach.

It's very much part of the local culture, and you can people-watch or have a picnic while working on the tan.

Exploring the 'Hoods. Many of Miami's districts have their own identity, depending on the locals who live in them. You'll want to see some of the city's famed diversity, from Little Havana (see page 54) to Coconut Grove (see page 74) and from the Brickell neighborhood south of Downtown (see page 67) all the way to North Miami (see page 42).

Eating a Cuban sandwich. Miami's diversity is also reflected in its food, and there are many specialties from Cuba and elsewhere in the Caribbean, Central America, and South America. You'll also want to sample the local seafood, with fresh crabs and lobster readily available. See page 16.

Having a 'Key experience'. Even if you don't rent a car and drive all the way to the southern tip of the Florida Keys (see page 84) you should at least explore the northernmost key, Key Biscayne, to get a feel for them (see page 72).

The inviting Crandon Park Beach, Key Biscayne

fall tends to be in short sharp bursts, often in the afternoons, after which the sun will come back out. The best time to come is from about January to April when it will be dry and with warm temperatures in the 70°Fs and 80°Fs (about 21°–32°C), perhaps a little cooler in January, and chilly at night. From October through to December you can still have a very pleasant vacation there, and certainly a cheaper one outside the high season, but it will be slightly cooler.

POPULATION

With a population of about 400,000 (downtown only), Miami is only the 44th biggest city in the US, so it punches well above its weight in terms of sta-

Calle Ocho in historic Little Havana

tus. But it does rank 7th in size if you take in the Greater Metropolitan Area. Almost 35 percent of that population is of Cuban descent, with a further 16 percent with roots in Central America, and 20 percent are African-American – a very diverse city indeed. It also has the reputation for being a city for retirees, which is true to a certain extent but they only represent a small proportion of the population. There are twice as many people under the age of 24 as there are over-65s.

LOCAL CUSTOMS

Although Florida is part of the South, it isn't really southern in the way that most people think of the term. Miami, being such a racially diverse city, is even less the southern stereotype. That said you will find the typical good manners and politeness that the South is noted for, and you should respond in kind.

One local quirk is that most restaurants will automatically add a tip to your bill, typically from about 12–15 percent. Watch out for this when paying as you could easily end up tipping twice. You can ask to amend the amount if you think it's too high or too low.

You should also always carry ID with you if you want to have a drink somewhere – it doesn't matter how old you are. Some places have strict policies to make sure they're not caught serving any of the many under-age visitors that flock here, especially during Spring Break.

'Gator in Shark Valley

Local reputation for being courteous stops when behind a steering wheel. Bar the elderly slow drivers, everyone else here is fast and reckless. People switch lanes without warning and often don't use their turn signals.

Thanks to the Latin influence, it's common in Miami to greet people with a European-style kiss, a *besito*, not common everywhere in the US. Another aspect of Latin behavior is a penchant for tardiness. Don't be surprised if you arrange to meet someone and they turn up half an hour late. It's also the norm for Miamians to eat later than their fellow Americans, so dinner at 8pm is much more common than dinner at 5pm.

Street artist in Wynwood

When it comes to the subject of Cuba, and Cuban politics (see below), feelings run strong and some people hold extreme views. It's best to avoid the topic if you're not sure what someone thinks, or you risk offending people.

POLITICS AND ECONOMICS

The city of Miami is governed by a mayor alongside five city commissioners, one from each of the city's main districts. The current mayor is Tomás Pedro Regalado, a member of the right-wing Republican Party who was born in Havana. He was elected in 2009 with 72 percent of the votes, and re-elected in 2013, this time winning 78 percent of the votes. He will have to step down in 2017 as the mayor is limited to two four-year terms, although commissioners have no such term limits.

Economically Miami is a city of extremes. It has a broad range of industries, including shipping, TV, its airport (one of the busiest in the US), and of course tourism. It also has a large number of people living in poverty. Although it did suffer during the recent financial crisis, it weathered the storm better than most thanks to this diverse economy. Miami is ranked as one of the richest cities in the US, and even in the world. The growth may well continue, depending on what happens in its relations with Cuba. If the opening up of relations continues, the city can expect to see its airport and port even busier.

The Seven Mile Bridge   *At Key West's Southernmost Point, Cuba is only 90 miles away*

Sun and heat. Make sure you wear sun cream at all times when outdoors, and not only when you're lying on the beach. You can get burned simply walking round the city, and the sun can be fierce. Even if it's overcast, some of the sun's rays are still coming through, so don't take a chance. It's also a good idea to wear a hat. The humidity means that you will sweat more, so drink lots of water to avoid dehydration.

Free art walks. There are several free art walks and open evenings at galleries around Miami. They include in the Wynwood neighborhood (see page 46) and adjoining Design District on the second Saturday evening of each month, and also in Coral Gables on the first Friday of each month.

Read hotel reviews. Before booking your Miami hotel check out reviews online and in this book (see page 92). Some of the beachfront hotels are notable for having party atmospheres, which are not conducive to a good night's sleep, especially at weekends. You may prefer to stay a block or two back from the ocean, or choose a more upscale hotel.

Free bike tour. In Coconut Grove there is a free historic cycling tour which sets out from City Hall at 9.30am on the first and third Saturdays of each month.

Big Night in Little Haiti. If you are in Little Haiti on the third Friday of the month, you can round your day off with a music concert. Big Night in Little Haiti takes place at the Little Haiti Cultural Center (212 NE 59 Terrace), starting at 6pm with a nominal donation request to cover the fun.

Free museum admissions. As is the case in many US cities, Miami has free admission to some of its museums, usually on one day per month. These include the Pérez Art Museum (second Saturdays 1–4pm), the Miami Children's Museum (third Fridays 3–9pm), the Wolfsonian-FIU (every Friday 6–9pm), and the Lowe Art Museum (first Tuesdays), while the Museum of Contemporary Art has free outdoor concerts on the last Friday of each month at 8pm.

Pack for comfort. Following the routes in this book you'll be doing a lot of walking, and maybe cycling, so make sure you have comfortable footwear, shorts and T-shirts. You should also allow for the humid climate: you'll be sweating a lot more, so plan a change of clothes for each day.

Check the calendar. Miami is a popular destination for conventions, festivals and other events (see page 23). If you're booking a trip there and find that flights and hotel rates seem to be high, it may be that you're coinciding with one of these major events. If you can be flexible on dates, check prices for a week or so either side, or contact your preferred hotel and ask them if there's an event on and when will room rates be cheaper.

Fried plantain is a popular side dish

FOOD AND DRINK

It's not all shrimp, alligator steaks, and Key lime pie. Miami's multi-ethnic population is reflected in its cuisine, and the strong Caribbean influences from Haiti, the Dominican Republic, and Cuba especially, all add their spice to the mix.

Miami, like the whole state of Florida, enjoys a cuisine based on fresh and locally-sourced fruit and vegetables, as well as an abundance of fresh fish. You'll find it to suit all budgets, from a thriving street food and food truck scene through to the very best in high-end restaurants.

LOCAL CUISINE

It's sometimes easy to forget that Florida is in the South, a region known for its fried chicken, barbecue sauce and grits. You will certainly find such southern food in Miami, but because of the city's many other culinary influences, it's a little less prevalent than elsewhere.

In Miami you're more likely to find a healthier diet based around seafood. One local seafood specialty is the Florida stone crab, favored for its sweet meat. They're not exclusive to Florida but hopefully yours will be locally caught. The crabs themselves are quite small but the claws are big and packed with meat. What's unusual about them is that their claws regrow if broken off, so often 'maimed' crabs are returned to the sea, and that's why you'll see more crab claws on menus than whole crabs.

Cuban cuisine

Of all the Caribbean flavors on offer in Miami, the Cuban influence prevails. During the late 19th century Cuban cigar makers began migrating to Key West, bringing with them the harbingers of a cuisine that has since spread across all of South Florida, especially Miami and its Little Havana neighborhood.

Cuban staples include *ropa vieja* (old clothes), a long-simmered stew of shredded beef; the slow-roasted pork called *lechón*; plantains fried in butter until they caramelize; and *picadillo*, a mélange of ground meat and potatoes seasoned with onions, tomatoes, pimientos, green olives, and capers. Black beans and rice are a universal accompaniment, and a mainstay throughout the day is strong Cuban coffee, usually well sweetened and served in the morning with hot milk as *café con leche*.

The one ubiquitous Cuban dish you can find everywhere, even without seeking out a Cuban restaurant, is the Cubano, or Cuban sandwich, stuffed with ham, roast pork, cheese, and pickles, served toasted. The *medianoche* version (a popular midnight snack hence its name) is made with a sweeter variety of bread that has a soft, flaky inside.

Seafood is plentiful

Stone crabs are a seasonal delicacy

Other Caribbean influences

The nearby Caribbean islands have contributed to the local cuisine. Thanks to a sizable Dominican community, Miami is a good place to try *pastelitos*, turnovers filled with meat or cheese, fish poached in coconut milk, or the hearty stew *sancocho*, made with chicken or beef mixed with green plantains, cassava (yucca), creamy yautia, and potatoes – invariably served with rice. For dessert, *buñuelos*, sweet dough balls, are a popular accompaniment to coffee.

From Jamaica come spicy meat pasties (also called turnovers) and jerk chicken and pork, the time-honored street foods of Kingston and Montego Bay, along with curried goat, chicken, and shrimp. The tamarind and ginger native to the island season many Jamaican dishes, and cassava bread is always a favorite.

Haitians, one of the most recent immigrant groups, have brought their fondness for fish boiled with lime juice, onion and garlic, and hot pepper. Highly seasoned beef patties and corn fritters are also reminders of their creole cuisine. Unlike Cubans, Haitians prepare their rice with red beans, not black. Cooks from northern Haiti spice their bean sauce with cloves. Whole snapper is fried, or cooked in a light tomato sauce with onions.

A taste of South America

Hispanic Miami is not only Caribbean. The city's large Nicaraguan population has opened numerous restaurants serving steak, grilled and served with a pungent chimichurri sauce, made from parsley and garlic. Another dish is *pescado a la Tipitapa*, a deep-fried red snapper drenched in an onion and pepper sauce.

Several North Beach Argentinian and South American restaurants also satisfy the beef-lovers' palate. The *parillada* is a treasure trove of meats hot off the grill – steak, chorizo, blood sausage, sweetbreads.

Key lime pie

You won't want to eat Key lime pie every day, though you should try it at least once of course: and they make a good one at Joe's Stone Crab in South Beach (see page 99). The name comes from the Key limes found in the Florida Keys, so you might want to save it if you plan to take a drive through the Keys (see page 84). Don't let it spoil your enjoyment, but most of the Key limes these days are imported from Mexico. The traditional version comes with a meringue topping made with the whites from the eggs whose yolks are used in the pie filling, along with the lime juice and sweetened condensed milk. These days you also find them served topped with cream or ice-cream instead. Originally the filling wasn't baked, as the lime juice, egg yolks and condensed milk combined and thickened naturally, but because raw egg yolks be problematic for some people, today's pies are cooked just a little, unless the menu says otherwise.

Food trucks in Miami Beach

With sexy samba beating in the background, try the Brazilian national dish, *feijoada*, a slow-cooked black bean stew full of juicy pork loin and smoked sausage and accompanied by *farofa*, which is sautéed ground yucca.

Sustainable seafood

Given the extensive variety of seafood on Miami menus, it's a good idea to be aware of which species are relatively abundant and which have suffered from fishing pressure. Grouper is a long-lived species that is particularly vulnerable to overfishing, and management of the fishery has been spotty. Orange roughy also have long reproductive cycle – they don't mature until 20 years old – and their stocks have been significantly depleted by trawler fishing, which also damages their deep-water spawning habitat. Sharks, too, are slow-growing and do not reproduce prolifically, and they are heavily overfished in international waters.

Among the least threatened commercially caught fish is mahi-mahi, which reproduces quickly and can sustain high fishing pressure – especially when the trolling method is used and not longline fishing. Albacore, yellowfin, and skipjack tuna stocks also stand up to commercial harvest, as long as pole and troll methods are used; longline and purse-seine fishing for tuna takes a heavy toll and causes the collateral destruction of sharks.

Among sustainable shellfish species, Florida hard clams are a particular standout. The clams, which are farmed commercially off Brevard County on the Atlantic and along the Gulf Coast, grow to maturity in suspended nets, which eliminates the need for harmful dredging, and do not require feeding with fishmeal or other potential pollutants, as the mollusks filter nutrients from seawater.

WHERE TO EAT

From street food stalls to award-winning restaurants, dining options in Miami cover all the bases. Obviously if you want to sample the best Cuban cuisine, spend a night in Little Havana, while Little Haiti will show you what Haitian cuisine is all about with storefront restaurants where just a couple of dollars will get you a plate of beans and rice, fried plantains and *griot* – fried pork chunks – to fill you up for the rest of the day.

You don't have to spend to get the best food either. It's true that you could easily empty your wallet if you choose the biggest and best crab at Joe's Stone Crab (see page 99) in South Beach, one of Miami's most famous restaurants, but you can equally enjoy the atmosphere and just have a salad or sandwich.

If you're looking for gourmet dining then start your search by considering the high-end hotels and resorts. You don't need to be a resident to eat in them, and they have the clout and the cash to attract some of the best chefs, even if sometimes only in a supervisory role. Look to places like the Biltmore Hotel (see page 103), and the Fontainebleau (see page 98).

The News Café, an Ocean Drive institution

Everglades fare

If modern Miami is an international buffet, old Miami is distinctly more Dixie. For the real roots, look towards the Everglades. Of the indigenous creatures found in early Miami, the alligator was the only plausibly edible inhabitant and it now appears on local menus, especially the tail, all lean white meat, and often described like tasting like chicken.

Venturing into the swamps, the fires of Miami native Americans – the Miccosukee Indians – can sometimes be seen. Their fried bread is a delicacy.

DRINKS

Florida is hardly noted for its wine production, although there are a couple of dozen or so wineries dotted around the state. You should certainly try some Florida wines if given the chance, although wine lists will be more focused on the wines of California and the world's other major wine regions. Florida wine-making does in fact go all the way back to the 16th century when the Spanish missionaries grew grapes to make communion wine. The state doesn't have a natural grape-growing climate, though, so many wineries today use hybrid grapes especially created to cope with the hot and humid climate, while some winemakers are using tropical fruits. The results can be interesting – just don't expect Burgundy.

In this hot climate, fruit juices and smoothies are popular, and so are long cocktails. You won't have to drive to Jimmy Buffet's Margaritaville in Key West to find a margarita, and Miami's Cuban connections also mean there's a ready supply of mojitos, daiquiris and, of course, Cuba libres. There are more adventurous cocktails too, as local mixologists produce new and unusual combinations of flavors.

Also welcome in the hot Miami climate are cool, refreshing beers. Florida, like many states, has a thriving craft brewing scene, with over 110 craft breweries currently in operation. In Miami look for names like Panagra, Wynwood, Wakefield, and Concrete Beach Brewery.

Florida citrus

The orange is emblematic of Florida, and appears on the state's number plates. That said oranges are not native to Florida: they were brought to the peninsula by the Spanish explorers Ponce de León and Hernando de Soto and soon grew wild.

The orange industry in Florida got its start as early as the 1770s. A century later, thousands of acres of groves had been planted, and Florida oranges were heading north by train just as the tourists were traveling south. The region around the Indian River (not a river but a saltwater lagoon) became a prime growing area.

Indian River is also famous for its grapefruit, a citrus family member that originated in the West Indies and was first planted in Florida in 1823. Shipments of grapefruit didn't reach the northeastern US until the 1880s, when Americans began to develop a taste for them.

Trendy fashions and décor at The Webster, on Collins Avenue

SHOPPING

If you're a shopoholic, welcome to Miami. You could spend your entire vacation visiting the city's shopping malls and stores, where you'll find everything from kitsch to classy fashion and contemporary crafts.

Bling and bliss, glamor and great bargains: Miami is a shopper's paradise. In an open-air city, cool clothes are second only to naked skin in the 'look-at-me' sweepstakes.

If money is no object, try the Village of Merrick Park in Coral Gables. Alternatively visit the elegant Bal Harbour Shops, where restaurants will even feed your poodle. If design is your thing, head to the Wynwood Art District or the Design District, and overindulge in the attitude. The Design District has been undergoing an extensive renovation and expansion – once the realm of showrooms featuring furniture, antiques, accessories, and art catering to interior decorators and their clients, it now includes the red-heeled beauties of Christian Louboutin and fashion-forward Maison Martin Margiela.

For those looking for more cultural souvenirs of Miami to bring back home, all neighborhoods have their own art galleries and crafts stores. Little Havana and Little Haiti both boast a colorful array of local stores (including cigar stores) as well as food stalls, where the local *croquetas* make for the perfect pit-stop snack.

SHOPPING MALLS

There are myriad shopping malls scattered all over Miami's greater metropolitan area. Most are open seven days a week and offer entertainment, too. Too many to mention by name here are our top recommendations.

Aventura Mall. The locals' favorite and also the largest mall in Florida. With 300 stores to choose from there is something for everyone, and for every budget. Movie buffs will also appreciate its 24-screen theater.

Lincoln Road Mall. South Beach's pedestrian retail center has outdoor restaurants, galleries and great opportunities for people-watching. Here you'll find independent stores like Alchemist but also newcomers like fitness brand Lululemon and Parisian favorite Zadig & Voltaire. There is also a farmer's market Sundays 9am–6.30pm.

Bal Harbour Shops. High-end boutiques (think Chanel and Saint Laurent but also trend-setter Isabel Marant) and charming cafés in a lush, luxurious setting.

Village of Merrick Park. A Mediterranean-style village, complete with garden and

Art Deco–inspired jewelry

fountains, catering for the ladies who lunch in Coral Gables.

ARTS AND CRAFTS

It can be a surprise to some visitors, who expect beaches, sunshine and nightlife, to find that places like Miami (and Orlando is another example) have thriving arts and craft scenes. The city has numerous art galleries showcasing the latest local art for sale, and international artists too. Several areas have art walks once a month or so, when galleries will stay open late and lay on wine or entertainment for visitors, to encourage them to buy.

Districts like North Miami (see page 42), South Beach (see page 36), and the Wynwood neighborhood (see page 46) are especially prolific in art galleries and craft stores. So too, and more colorful, are Little Haiti and Little Havana (see page 54). Both those neighborhoods make great places to walk around, even if you're only window shopping.

ART DECO SOUVENIRS

Renowned for its Art Deco hotels and other buildings, there is of course a wealth of Art Deco souvenirs for you to choose from. They (mostly) make for gifts that are a little more tasteful than the usual holiday memento. Art Deco-style jewelry can be very appealing, and a good idea if you don't have much room in your baggage. Cheaper options include posters, coasters, and T-shirts. There are plenty of books, too, including some wonderful coffee table books showing the main Art Deco buildings in all their glory.

Outdoor stalls on Lincoln Road

The Art Deco Tower Theater in Little Havana

ENTERTAINMENT

Miami may have an image as a city for partying holidaymakers and retirees, but there are lots of cultural attractions like opera, movies, dance, and drama, alongside the rowdier nightlife in the clubs and bars.

Cinema is a particular attraction in Miami, a city that not only stars in numerous movies but where people love to watch them too. There's a big enough local population to sustain drama, dance, comedy, opera, classical music, and ballet companies, without having to rely on the tourist dollar. As such, visitors are often surprised to discover just what a thriving and eclectic entertainment scene there is.

CINEMA

Miami plays host to the Miami International Film Festival, which draws more than 60,000 movie buffs every year. A showcase for exciting documentary, drama and shorts, each February MIFF shows films from as many as 47 countries. There's also the Miami Independent Film Festival, and some of the movie houses and colleges run film festivals or special seasons of their own. If you're into movies, Miami will not disappoint. Nor will some of the places they're shown in, as some of the local cinemas were built during the city's Art Deco architecture boom, and are still going strong, making a movie outing something of an occasion. There are also numerous multiplex cinemas where to enjoy the blockbusters (see page 104).

The Magic City is a modern-day frontier town, painted with tropical colors and air-brushed with urban grit. It's a steamy location for tales of lawbreakers, jet-setters and cross-dressers. Miami's unique and well-preserved architecture also plays its part and there are myriad Miami tours catering to *Dexter* and *Miami Vice* aficionados.

THEATER

There are Art Deco theaters still in business too, with some having turned into movie houses, and some movie houses having turned into theaters over the years. The Colony Theater and the Jackie Gleason Theater (now the Fillmore Miami Beach, see page 107) are just two places where your surroundings will impress as much as what's on stage. And what is on stage could be anything from the latest Broadway shows to musical revivals to experimental theater to Shakespeare and the classics.

The Adrienne Arsht Center   *Live music at the Hoy Como Ayer nightclub*

All art forms are showcased at the Adrienne Arsht Center for the Performing Arts (see page 63), the largest performing arts center in the country outside of New York. Miami has its own Miami New Drama group, whose home is the Colony Theater, while lighter offerings can often be found at the Waterfront Theater (see page 107), the largest theater in the state.

DANCE

The Miami City Ballet is one name to watch for, and they perform at the Adrienne Arsht Center for the Performing Arts. Recent sold-out successes have been productions of *Gisele* and *The Nutcracker*.

For more contemporary work look to the South Miami–Dade Cultural Arts Center or the New World Center (see page 107). Also worth seeking out are Miami companies showcasing international dance such as the Ballet Flamenco La Rosa and IFÉ-ILÉ Afro-Cuban Dance and Music.

ROCK AND POP

You might be lucky enough to catch a concert by one of the big names like Adele or Sting, but if not then you're still guaranteed good music every night of the week whether your taste is for blues, jazz, rock, Latin American, folk or anything else. Check out our listings on page 105.

CLASSICAL MUSIC AND OPERA

Miami is the home for the Florida Grand Opera, who perform at the Adrienne Arsht Center for the Performing Arts, while the New World Symphony Orchestra base themselves at the Frank Gehry-designed New World Center in South Beach.

NIGHTLIFE

You can party long and hard in Miami, if that's your thing, as the city has several vast state-of-the-art nightclubs (see page 106). There are more intimate clubs, music clubs covering all genres and, of course, bars galore from swanky to dive.

Festivals

It's worth trying to time your visit to coincide with one of Miami's annual art festivals. Film buffs should look for the dates of the Miami International Film Festival in the spring, and round about the same time is Florida's largest arts festival in Coconut Grove. Little Havana's carnival season also runs around then. At other times of the year there are wine and food festivals, a book festival (one of the biggest and liveliest gatherings on the US literary calendar), and a one-day celebration of Caribbean culture by way of the Miami Broward Carnival in October (see page 111 for full details of all festivals).

The Hialeah Park Race Track featured in the opening credits of Miami Vice

OUTDOOR ACTIVITIES

Like most places blessed with a good climate, Miami embraces the great outdoors, and as well as what happens in the city itself there's a wealth of outdoor opportunities on the doorstep, from the Everglades to numerous parks.

The outdoor adventures can be as soft or as tough as you like, on the land or on the sea – or even under it, with scuba diving one of the many ocean activities on offer. There are plenty of beach and water sports, bike-riding, hiking, tennis and other sports, with many options suitable for families.

CYCLING

Miami is a bike-friendly city, and renting a bike is a good way to get around. You can even go bike riding in the Everglades (see page 79). There are also a number of organized bike tours.

An impressive catch

PARKS

In Miami you expect the high-rise buildings and the Art Deco architecture. What you don't expect are the numerous parks dotted around the city. Residents make full use of them, so visitors should check them out as well, even if you want nothing more than an early morning jog. Different parks obviously have different facilities. One of the most popular, thanks to being right by the ocean, is Lummus Park in the Deco district of South Beach. Don't be surprised if you see a film crew there as it's a popular shooting location. Facilities here include hiking and biking trails, volleyball, fitness equipment, and kids' activities.

There are more ocean views at Peacock Park and the Alice C. Wainwright Park, both in Coconut Grove, the latter boasting basketballs courts and an outdoor gym too. If you're traveling with children head for the Historic Virginia Key Beach Park with its carousel, mini train and other activities. And an ocean view, of course. For a real slice of Miami life go to Domino Park in Little Havana, where you'll see the locals hanging out and shooting the breeze.

Airboat tour near Shark Valley

GOLF

Miami has the perfect climate for golf, and with about 40 courses within 20 miles of the city center, you're spoilt for choice if you want to practise your swing. One of the best, and closest, is the Westview Country Club, while the Trump National Doral Golf Club has an impressive four courses.

HORSE RACING

West of the city, the Hialeah Park Racing and Casino offers horse-racing enthusiasts the chance to watch a race at one of the country's most respected tracks, as well as enjoy the park gardens and the casino (see page 104). If you're staying on the north side then there's another racetrack/casino combo at the Gulfstream Park Racetrack and Casino. The racetrack has been in business since 1939, while the casino boasts 17 restaurants, so you won't go hungry provided you don't lose your shirt on the horses first.

TENNIS

The Crandon Park International Tennis Center has 26 courts, of which seven are illuminated for night playing, and there are other venues if you want to take advantage of the Miami climate and play or take lessons. These include Flamingo Park in Miami Beach and Tropical Park out in Westchester.

WILDLIFE

You don't have to travel far from the center of Miami to spot wildlife. Just south of the city is the Biscayne National Park, where can spot lizards, iguanas, foxes, bobcats, and toads. The park was originally going to be part of the Everglades National park but plans changed. The Everglades is the big one for wildlife, of course, and here you'll probably see deer and gators, maybe bobcats, foxes, otters, turtles, terrapins… and be warned there are plenty of snakes. What you probably won't see is the endangered Florida panther, as only about 100 remain in southern Florida.

WATER SPORTS

Deep-sea fishing is a popular diversion in Miami, and it's big business too with many boats going from Key Biscayne. You can book half-day or full-day trips, with the full-day options obviously giving you more chance to get out further and maybe land a bigger fish. Bring a sun hat.

If you want to be out on the ocean but don't care about the fishing, you can take a speedboat tour out through the bays, and that can get the adrenaline going. You can also rent your own boat and make your own adventure, or try jet skis too. A little safer but still a lot of fun is to take an airboat tour on the Everglades. There are countless options available, and you're sure to see some kind of wildlife.

The Florida East Coast Railway to Miami, 1896

HISTORY: KEY DATES

The history of Miami is inevitably mixed in with the history of Florida, and a fascinating story it is, involving the first Native American settlers, European arrivals, the Civil War and the making and breaking of ties with Cuba.

PRE-HISTORY

c.8000 BC	Nomadic tribes reach the Florida peninsula and begin to settle the land a few thousand years later.
600–500 BC	Native Americans settle near the mouth of the Miami River.

EUROPEAN ARRIVALS

1513	Spanish conquistador Ponce de León is the first European to set foot on the peninsula, near present-day St Augustine. He later returns to Biscayne Bay and present-day Miami with settlers, but abandons his expedition.
1562	The French arrive in Florida to challenge the Spanish, who then strengthen their hold, founding their first permanent settlement three years later.
1567	First Spanish mission built in what is now Miami.
1586	A British attack on St Augustine triggers centuries of dispute between Britain, France, and Spain, and America.
1763	The English receive Florida from Spain in exchange for Cuba. Twenty years later, the territory is returned to Spain.
1803	The Spanish cede Florida's Panhandle to Napoleon, who soon sells the region to the United States.

THE FORMING OF FLORIDA

1817–18	Pressure from settlers results in violence with Indian tribes and leads to the outbreak of the First Seminole War. Andrew Jackson overcomes Seminole resistance, then sets about taking control of Florida on behalf of the US government. He becomes Florida's first governor, and later US president.

Miami Beach in 1957

1824	The newly founded town of Tallahassee is declared the capital of the Florida Territory.
1835–42	Seminole leader Osceola launches a campaign against the US Army which ends when most Indians surrender and are deported.
1845	Florida becomes the 27th state of the Union.
1861	Florida secedes from the Union and joins the Confederate States in the Civil War.
1868	Following a revolt against Spain in Cuba, the first wave of Cubans arrives in Florida.
1883	The great railroad era begins. Settlers head south.
1896	Miami incorporated as a city with a population of just a few hundred.
1898	Revolution erupts in Cuba; the US joins in to drive Spain off the island.

THE 20TH CENTURY

1912	Completion of the final section of the East Coast Railroad to Key West, prompting the first property boom of the 20th century and raising the state's population to one million people.
1926–28	Two powerful hurricanes strike Miami, killing over 2,000 people.
1930s–40s	Miami Beach's Art Deco hotels are built and tourism thrives in South Florida. During World War II Florida is used as a training ground for soldiers.
1959	Fidel Castro leads a communist revolution in Cuba, setting off a long-term migration of thousands of Cubans who flee his regime, particularly to Miami. More *emigrés* from Central and South America follow.
1980s	The campaign to restore the Art Deco district of Miami Beach launches the area's renaissance.
1984	The influential TV series *Miami Vice* premieres, changing the public image of the city.
1992	Hurricane Andrew devastates southeast Florida.
1997	Designer Gianni Versace is shot and killed in South Beach.
2004	Four hurricanes pummel the coastline over a 48-day period, breaking a record set in 1964.
2013	Celebrations of the 500th anniversary of the arrival in Florida of Ponce de León.
2016	Commercial flights resume between Miami International Airport and Havana, Cuba.

BEST ROUTES

The iconic Essex House Hotel

MIAMI BEACH ART DECO HOTELS

This short walking tour shows you why Miami is the finest city in the US for Art Deco architecture, with many grand hotels that have survived from the 1930s and 40s and are now protected buildings.

DISTANCE: 1.5 miles (2.4km)
TIME: 2–3 hours with stops
START: Art Deco Welcome Center
END: Miami Beach Visitors Center
POINTS TO NOTE: Don't be nervous about walking into the hotels mentioned here, and having a good look round. These are also historic buildings and the hotels are quite used to visitors wandering in and taking photos. A good time to do the walk is in the early afternoon, when hotel guests will have checked out of their rooms but new ones won't yet be checking in. It means the staff will have more time to answer any questions you might have.

Miami Beach has over 500 Art Deco buildings, most of them in the South Beach part of the city, and many of them hotels. They make fabulous places to stay, of course, but you can't stay in all of them so don't miss the chance to see as many of them as you can – inside and outside. This walk is just a taster of some of the more interesting hotels that

are reasonably close together, but there are many more dotted around the city.

The best of the hotels date back to the 1930s and 40s, when the city of Miami experienced a financial boom in various industries including tourism. People had money to invest in building the best hotels – although not always from legal businesses! They recruited the best architects from all over the country to design those hotels. Fortunately for us, the favored architectural style of the time was Art Deco, one of the more aesthetically pleasing periods of American architecture, though you don't need to know anything about architecture to enjoy this walk.

WELCOME CENTER

Begin the tour at the **Art Deco Welcome Center** ❶ (tel: 305-672-2014; www. mdpl.org/welcome-center/visitors-center; daily 9.30am–7pm), run by the Miami Design Protection League. This is where you'll find anything you need to know about Art Deco, and it's also a visitor center for the overall Art Deco

The Clevelander's outdoor bar is party central

district. The Art Deco Museum inside displays scale models of some of the more significant buildings. You'll also learn about other architectural styles featured in the city – yes, it doesn't stop at Art Deco – notably Mediterranean Revival and Miami Modern, or MiMo.

The Essex House Hotel

One of the closest Art Deco hotels is the impressive **Essex House Hotel** (tel: 305-534-2700; www.clevelander.com)

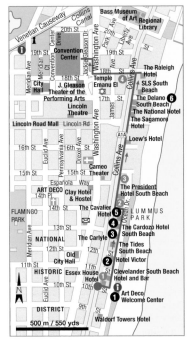

whose full name is now Essex House by Clevelander. To get there from the Welcome Center, cross over Ocean Drive and walk down 10th Street, almost opposite you. The Essex House is at the junction with Collins Avenue. The name Essex House features prominently on the facade, and the local architectural rules dictate that the name has to stay there, even if the hotel is bought by someone else. It can be confusing, and on some hotels you'll see two names. There will be the original name, which has to remain, and the new name, which can be added, though rules are strict about how that is done.

Built in 1938, the Essex was designed by Henry Hohauser, who is regarded as one of the very best Art Deco architects. The lobby is a sight to behold. Over the fireplace is an Everglades mural. These were popular in Art Deco hotels but not many survive. The bar here used to be a casino, and one notable regular there was Al Capone.

OCEAN DRIVE

Return to Ocean Drive and turn left to head north along Miami Beach's famous oceanfront thoroughfare. Almost immediately on the left is **The Clevelander** (tel: 305-532-4006; www.clevelander. com). Built in 1938, the hotel got its name from the original owners, who hailed from Cleveland. The exterior is stylishly simple and couldn't be more of a contrast to the Essex House, a clear

The Cardozo, another Henry Hohauser gem

example that not all Art Deco hotels are the same. This one is more of a party hotel for over 21s, and it's known for its bar as much as anything. Its Rock Star Suites are at the luxury end of the Miami Beach scale.

Walk north along Ocean Drive and if you're feeling hungry turn left on 11th Street and a short way along on your left is **Mom's New York Pizza**, see ❶. Otherwise keep going north on Ocean Drive and just before the junction with 12th Street is one of the city's finest hotels, **Hotel Victor** ❷ (tel: 305-779-8700; http://hotelvictorsouthbeach.com). The Victor was built in 1937 under the direction of architect L. Murray Dixon, who designed so many classic Art Deco hotels he became known as the Dean of Deco. The exterior is quite simple but inside many of the original Art Deco features have been preserved, including the original terrazzo flooring, and another example of an Everglades mural. Outside the pool area also reflects its 1930s heyday, and the hotel has featured in many episodes of the famous 1980s TV series, *Miami Vice*.

The Diva of Ocean Drive

Beyond 12th Street is **The Tides South Beach** (tel: 305-604-5070; www.tides southbeach.com). When The Tides was built in 1936 it was the tallest building in the city, and one of the highest in the whole of Florida. The lobby has incredibly high ceilings, supported by soaring columns. This was the first Art Deco build-ing in Miami to be designed by L. Murray Dixon. Nicknamed the Diva of Ocean Drive, it earned the architect many more commissions including The Ritz, The Tudor, The Tiffany, and Hotel Victor.

Continue walking north and the last building on this block, at the junction with 13th Street, is **The Carlyle** ❸ (tel: 305-531-3238; www.carlyleoceandrive. com). Built in 1939, the Carlyle's exterior has been virtually untouched ever since and its neon sign has featured in myriad fashion shoots, TV shows and movies, including Brian de Palma's *Scarface*. Unfortunately the interior retains few Art Deco features.

Art Deco Cuban-style

On the other side of 13th Street is **The Cardozo** ❹ (tel: 305-535-6500; www.cardozohotel.com), owned by the Cuban-born singer Gloria Estefan and her husband Emilio. The interior has a strong Cuban/Caribbean look to it, while the outside retains its Art Deco features. Built in 1939, it was designed by Art Deco maestro Henry Hohauser, also behind the Essex House, The Colony Hotel and Park Central Miami Beach. The Cardozo featured in the 1959 Frank Capra comedy, *A Hole in the Head*, and this is where Ben Stiller stayed in *There's Something About Mary*.

Next to The Cardozo is another Art Deco classic, **The Cavalier** ❺ (tel: 305-673-1199; www.cavaliersouthbeach. com), designed by Roy France. Apart from regular maintenance it appears

The Tides' elegant lobby　　　　　　　*The Carlyle Hotel, a fashion shoot favorite*

just as it was when it was built in 1936, and for this reason it has also featured in countless movies and TV shows. Inside it has the original terrazzo floor and a striking black and gold décor, along with typical Art Deco stained glass and lamps. Some of the guest rooms have these features too, but you'll have to stay there to see them for yourself.

COLLINS AVENUE

At the next junction you can grab a bite to eat at **Il Bolognese**, see ❷, on the far side of 14th Street. If you're not hungry then walk west along 14th Street and take the second right to walk north along Collins Avenue, another major Miami Beach thoroughfare which parallels Ocean Drive. A short way along on the right is **The President** (tel: 305-534-9334; www.presidentsouthbeach.com), one of the smaller Art Deco hotels, built in 1936 and designed by L. Murray Dixon. Because of its size there isn't a lot to see inside, though the reception area does have a crystal chandelier, as do the guest rooms. It was converted into an apartment building for about fifty years, then turned back into a hotel; many original features were retained, being covered over rather than ripped out and destroyed.

If you want a break from all the Art Deco, or even just a coffee, continue north on Collins Avenue through the Crowne Plaza Hotel to its **Front Porch Café**, see ❶. Otherwise stay on Col-

lins and on the right after the junction with Lincoln Road are several more Art Deco masterpieces. First is the **Sagamore Miami Beach** (tel: 305-535-8088; www.sagamorehotel.com) which also houses an art gallery. It's rather dwarfed by the next building along, **The National** (tel: 305-532-2311; http://nationalhotel.com). Designed by Roy

What Is Art Deco?

After a few hours in Miami Beach you'll certainly know what Art Deco looks like, but where did the style come from? It doesn't just apply to architecture but to art, jewelry, furniture, fashions, and even trains and cars. It came out of an exhibition in Paris in 1925 called the Exposition Internationale des Arts Décoratifs et Industriels Modernes (International Exhibition of Modern Decorative and Industrial Arts), whose artists combined a futuristic style with many artistic influences from the past, such as Cubism. They also believed in employing the best craftsmanship and using the best materials, and the style caught on in Europe and then spread to New York, especially in its skyscraper designs. From there it was a natural hop to Miami, a popular vacation spot with New Yorkers. The fact that it coincided with an economic boom in the city helped enormously, and Miami's Art Deco hotels were born.

The Delano and The National, side-by-side on Collins Avenue

France and opened in 1940, for many years The national was the place to stay in Miami Beach, and boasted the longest (203ft/62m) swimming pool in Florida. It's still the longest infinity pool in Miami, and worth walking through to the back of the hotel to take a look at.

Right next door is **The Delano South Beach** ❻ (tel: 305-672-2000; www.morganshotelgroup.com/delano/delano-south-beach). Built in 1947, the hotel was named after US President Franklin Delano Roosevelt, who had passed away two years earlier and was that unusual thing, a popular politician. It was renovated in 1994 under designer Philippe Starck's meticulous eye. The result is a remarkable interior, adorned by many original artworks, notably by Man Ray and Salvador Dalí. The Delano is where celebrities either stay or come to have drinks so you may well bump into Madonna, Justin Timberlake, J-Lo, Beyoncé, or George Clooney.

Further north on Collins Avenue, on the far side of 17th Street is **SLS South Beach** (tel: 305-674-1701; http://slshotels.com/southbeach), the tallest Art Deco building in South Beach at 12 floors high. When it was built in 1949 it was the first hotel in the city to have air-conditioning. It was originally designed by L. Murray Dixon, and later received a makeover courtesy of Philippe Starck, with the help of the musician Lenny Kravitz. It's a perfect example of what can be done with the interior of an Art Deco hotel, while maintaining the original exterior. Inside is all Starck-style while outside, if you look up to the top of the building, you'll see the inscription Ritz Plaza, the name of the hotel from 1946 until 2004, and even though it then acquired a new name, the original has to be kept on the outside.

Continuing north along Collins Avenue and the last building on this block, at the junction with 18th Street, is **The Raleigh** (tel: 305-534-6300; http://raleighhotel.com). Built in 1940, this is another L. Murray Dixon At Deco creation. But the inauguration glitz was short-lived: no sooner than it had opened, it had to close as a hotel so it could be used to house troops serve as the US Government's administrative headquarters during World War II. This happened to a lot of Miami's buildings, including other hotels, as the city was an important port for getting US troops to Europe. After the war it reopened as a kosher hotel, to cater to the city's many Jewish visitors. The ballroom even became a synagogue, though it's now a ballroom again. If you walk through the hotel to the swimming pool you'll see it still has its graceful Art Deco look – no wonder *Life Magazine* called it 'the most beautiful pool in America'.

Opposite the Raleigh on Collins Avenue is the small Redbury Hotel, whose **Cleo South Beach** restaurant, see ❹, is a great place to rest your feet and enjoy dinner.

The fabulously curvy 1940s pool at The Raleigh

Miami Beach Convention Center

A short diversion from the Art Deco tour, walking west along 18th Street (away from The Raleigh), is the **Miami Beach Convention Center** (tel: 786-276-2600; www.miamibeachconvention.com).

Although not Art Deco it still is an interesting building in its own right, having hosted such illustrious figures as Dr Martin Luther King Jnr, who delivered a speech here, and Muhammad Ali, who, as Cassius Clay, beat Sonny Liston here to become World Heavyweight Champion at the age of 22. It's also hosted the Republican National Convention in 1968, and then in 1971 it hosted both the Republican and the Democrat National Conventions. The Convention Center is set to get even bigger as it's undergoing a major $515 million renovation, though it's still operational and is expected to reopen fully in 2018.

Food and Drink

① MOM'S NEW YORK PIZZA

1059 Collins Ave #106, tel: 305-397-8844; www.momsnypizza.com; daily L and D; $$

New York pizza in Miami? Yes, when it's as good as Mom's, which stays open till 6am on Friday and Saturday. Mom's Supreme Pizza is pricey but would feed an army, so bring a hearty appetite.

② IL BOLOGNESE

1400 Ocean Drive; tel: 305-455-0399; www.ilbolognese.com; daily B, L and D; $$

This smart but friendly restaurant takes a sophisticated take on the hearty food of northern Italy, with chef Manuel Mattei hailing from Bergamo. There's a risotto of the day and dishes such as lamb *osso bucco*, but American dishes too like steaks and Maine lobster.

③ THE FRONT PORCH CAFÉ

1458 Ocean Drive; tel: 305-531-8300; www.frontporchoceandrive.com; daily B, L and D; $$

This relaxed place offers all-day dining, whether you want a full meal or simply a coffee or a classy cocktail in the Breezeway Bar. Organic ingredients are used wherever possible in dishes ranging from a salmon sandwich to New York strip or their specialty meatloaf.

④ CLEO SOUTH BEACH

The Redbury South Beach, 1776 Collins Avenue; tel: 305-534-2536; http://theredbury.com/southbeach/eat_drink/cleo; daily B, L and D; $$$

Israeli chef Danny Elmaleh brings Middle Eastern/Mediterranean flair to this hip hotel's highly-rated smart-casual restaurant, serving starters such as *baba ganoush* or *dolmades*, and spicy main courses including couscous or spicy Moroccan fish tagine.

Colorful art at Britto Central

SOUTH BEACH ART WALK

*Miami is an artsy city, with many neighborhoods boasting
excellent galleries, notably around Lincoln Road in South Beach.
This short route takes you to some of the area's best art showcase.*

DISTANCE: 2 miles (3.2km)
TIME: 1 hour without stops
START: Britto Central
END: World Erotic Art Museum
POINTS TO NOTE: If you are in Miami
in December, check out the Miami Art
Project (http://miami-project.com) and
Aqua Art Miami (www.aquaartmiami.com).
On the first Saturday of each month the
galleries around Lincoln Road stay open
late as part of the Saturday Night Art Walk.

South Beach isn't just all about Art Deco.
The area also has a thriving contemporary art scene, with galleries displaying
buoyant and colorful local art. There's a
particular vibrancy about the output of
second- or third-generation Cuban and
Caribbean American artists.

LINCOLN ROAD

Start the tour at **Britto Central** ❶ (1102
Lincoln Rd Mall; tel: 305-531-8821; www.
britto.com; Sun–Wed 10am–10pm, Thu–
Sat 10am–11pm), one of the best art galleries along Lincoln Road, featuring the
work of Brazilian-born Romero Britto. It's
a fun treasure trove where you'll find anything from Disney collectibles to owl tea-
pots and striking iPad and iPhone covers.
One of several Britto outlets in Miami, this
one is at the Lincoln Road Mall, a pedes-
trianised cluster of stores, galleries and
eateries. For a bite to eat, head to Lenox
Avenue and **Juvia** restaurant, see ❶.

Otherwise continue east along the mall
to reach on the right-hand (south) side
the **ArtCenter South Florida** ❷ (924
Lincoln Road; tel: 305-674-8278; www.
artcentersf.org; Mon–Fri 11am–7pm,
Sat–Sun noon–8pm). A gallery, administrative center and artists' studios all-
in-one, it's an exciting place to visit no
matter what's going on. The center runs
art classes for local residents, and brings
in visiting artists to give classes and display their work. There are exhibitions
from their resident artists too.

Continue east along the mall and after
crossing Meridian Avenue on your left is
Peter Lik Miami (701 Lincoln Road; tel:
786-235-9570; www.lik.com/galleries/
miami.html; Sun–Thu 10am–11pm, Fri–

The all white and clean lines of the New World Center

Sat 10am–midnight), one of a worldwide chain of galleries featuring the works of the Australian landscape photographer. Opposite, the **Nexxt Café**, see ➋, is a good place for a post-gallery drink.

Further along the mall, turn left northwards on Pennsylvania Avenue, then right westwards on 17th Street. On your right is the **New World Center** ➌ (500 17th Street; tel: 305-673-3330; www.nws.edu), a concert hall designed by Frank Gehry (see page 107). Take a quick look inside before heading east through Soundscape Park all the way to Washington Avenue.

Down Washington Avenue, cross Lincoln Road on your right for the **David Castillo Gallery** (420 Lincoln Road; tel: 305-573-8110; http://davidcastillogall

ery.com; Tue–Wed and Fri–Sat 10am–6pm). This former warehouse turned art space has changing exhibitions showcasing striking contemporary works.

COLLINS AVENUE

Continue south on Washington Avenue, go left on 16th Street and right on Collins Avenue. On your left is the **Alexander Gore Art** (1501 Collins Avenue #205; tel: 305-672-8454; erratic opening hours). Gore is an artist who paints bold, abstract, expressionistic paintings. Right next door is **Quality Meats**, see ➌.

Keep south on Collins and turn right (west) on Española Way to **Mark Rutkowski Fine Arts** (405 Española Way #207; tel: 305-673-9713; http://markrutkowski. com), which is the artist's studio and is only open when he is about. Rutkowski's paintings feature his travels – and Miami of course. The Effusion Gallery also shows his work.

Continue south down Washington Avenue and on the east side is the **Look Beyond Art Gallery** (1427 Washington Avenue; tel: 786-431-9087; Sun–Thu 11am–10pm, Fri–Sat 11am–midnight), which looks like a pop art painting and sells equally bold and bright artworks.

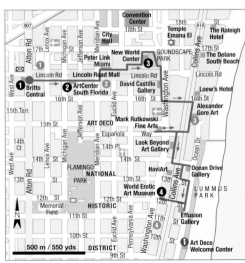

The World Erotic Art Museum, the only museum in the US devoted to erotic art

OCEAN DRIVE

Further south on Washington Avenue, turn left (east) on 14th Street and when you reach Ocean Drive on your right you'll see the **Ocean Drive Gallery** (1390 Ocean Drive; tel: 305-535-1511; phone for hours), a good place for pop art and fun souvenirs.

Go back to Collins Avenue, turn left to head south and on the other side of the street is the **HaviArt** gallery (1300 Collins Avenue; tel: 786-355-7087; www.haviart.com; variable opening hours), where Argentine-born Havi Schanz sells his remarkable portraits of celebrities past and present. You'll also find his work on show at the Carlyle Hotel (see page 32).

Go south on Collins and immediately east on 13th Street to return to Ocean Drive. Go south and past 12th Street and the Hotel Victor (see page 32) is the **Effusion Gallery** (1130 Ocean Drive; tel: 305-538-3558; www.effusiongallery.com; daily 10am–11pm) which has a wide range of fun items from pop art to pin-ups.

Go back west on 12th Street, and at the junction with Washington Avenue is the **World Erotic Art Museum** ❹ (1205 Washington Avenue; tel: 305-532-9336; http://weam.com; Mon–Thu 11am–10pm, Fri–Sun 11am–midnight), with a collection dating from 350BC to the present including works by Rembrandt, Picasso, Dalí and Botero, as well as photographers Robert Maplethorpe and Helmut Newton. If you're hungry then one block south on Washington is the **11th Street Diner**, see ❹.

Food and Drink

❶ JUVIA

1111 Lincoln Road; tel: 305-763-8272; www.juviamiami.com; Mon–Fri D, Sat–Sun L and D; $$$$

This upscale place combines French, Japanese and Peruvian cuisines, with a different chef for each style, be it duck foie gras terrine or wagyu short rib gyoza.

❷ NEXXT CAFÉ

700 Lincoln Road; tel: 305-532-6643; www.nexxtcafe.com; daily L and D; $$

This casual café with a huge seating area can cater for a simple coffee or a cocktail through to an elaborate lunch or dinner. The deluxe burgers are justifiably popular.

❸ QUALITY MEATS

1501 Collins Avenue; tel: 305-340-3333; www.qualitymeatsmiami.com; daily D; $$$$

Stylish restaurant cared out of a former hotel, so the check-in desk is now a butcher's counter, and naturally the food is meat-focused though they do serve seafood and lighter dishes too.

❹ 11TH STREET DINER

1065 Washington Avenue; tel: 305-534-6373; http://eleventhstreetdiner.com; Mon–Tue 7am–midnight, Wed–Sun 24h; $

Art Deco diner with classic booths and counter-seating; it has an all-day breakfast and takes no reservations. Weekend brunches see it packed.

Lummus Park's tree-lined promenade

SOUTH BEACH BY BIKE

Miami may be a bustling metropolis but it is also a bike-friendly one, with many popular bike trails, and this route shows how much more of the city you can see when you are on two wheels.

DISTANCE: 15 miles (24.1km)
TIME: 90 minutes without stops
START: Art Deco Welcome Center
END: South Pointe Pier
POINTS TO NOTE: You can rent bikes near the starting point of this tour. Allow time to return them if you're only renting for the day. Miami has a bike sharing scheme (http://citibikemiami.com), with about 100 stations around the city where bikes are available to use for a period of up to one hour, though you're going to need to rent a bike for longer to follow this route.

Miami used to be one of the worst cities in the US for cyclists, but the city has turned its reputation around and a recent poll ranked it the 8th most bike-friendly American city. There are shiny new bike paths and a bike-sharing scheme is now in place. For the visitor, bikes put much more of the city within reach; this route concentrates on South Beach but includes a hop across to Miami and back to show you the islands in Biscayne Bay and some views to take your breath away.

LUMMUS PARK

Start at the **Art Deco Welcome Center** ❶ (tel: 305-672-2014; www.mdpl.org/welcome-center/visitors-center; daily 9.30am–7pm). A short walk down 10th Street, is **Bike and Roll** (210 10th Street; tel: 305-604-0001; http://bikemiami.com; daily 8am–8pm), where you can rent bikes (or skates or Segways) for the day. Dust off your cycling legs in adjacent Lummus Park, whose palm trees have often featured in *Miami Vice*.

Many of the hotels on Ocean Drive on your left feature in Route 1 (see page 30) but look out for the **Casa Casuarina**, just north of 14th Street and set back from the road a little. Also known as the Versace Mansion, it was once the home of fashion designer Gianni Versace, who was murdered here, on the front steps, in 1997 by a serial killer. The villa is now a boutique hotel belonging to the Hotel Victor (see page 32).

Continue north through Lummus Park, exiting on the cycle pathway in the northeast corner, which runs behind the beach. The path emerges in a car park at the

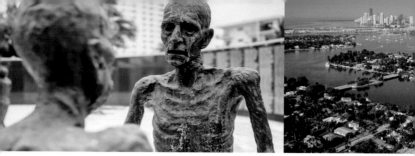

The evocative Holocaust Memorial

junction of 21st Street, where you turn left to go west along 21st Street. Cross the busy junction with Collins carefully and cycle into the park on the northwest corner. The large building at the western end of the park is **The Bass Museum of Art** (2100 Collins Avenue; tel: 305-673-7530; www.thebass.org), South Beach's main museum of contemporary art. Following a $12 million revamp the museum now has eight bright and spacious galleries housing works from North American, Latin American, Caribbean, and Asian artists. There are also sculptures and art installations both inside and in the grounds.

Gardens

Return to Collins Avenue and if you're hungry head north to **STK South Beach**, see ❶. Otherwise cycle south until you reach 17th Street. Turn right and go west along here, past the New World Center (see page 37) on your right. When you reach Meridian Avenue, turn right to cycle north. On your right after crossing 19th Street is the city's **Holocaust Memorial** (http://holocaustmemorialmiamibeach.org; daily 9.30am–10pm). This simple yet powerful sculpture is the inspiration of a group of holocaust survivors. It also provides a memorial garden for quiet contemplation and a memorial wall where thousands of names are etched.

To the east of the memorial is the **Miami Beach Botanical Garden** ❷ (2000 Convention Center Drive; tel: 305-673-7256; http://mbgarden.org; Tue–Sun 9am–5pm; donation), featuring native Florida plants, a Japanese Garden, a mangrove and wetland area, and an edible garden – a perfect little oasis.

THE ISLANDS

Go back south on Meridian and turn right to go west on 17th Street. This takes you all the way to Miami and the mainland, going through the **Venetian Islands** ❸, a series of eleven manmade islands linked by the Venetian Causeway, built in 1927. This is where the rich and famous live –all year or just come down for the winter. After crossing the last of the islands, **Biscayne Island**, you're back on the mainland's 15th Street. Turn left onto Bayshore Drive, cross 14th Street and turn left again on 13th Street to

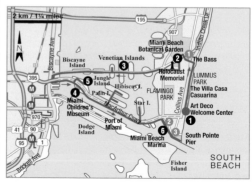

The Venetian Islands   *South Pointe Park at sunset*

head east back towards Miami Beach, this time on the MacArthur Causeway.

The first island you reach is Watson Island and on the right of the causeway is the **Miami Children's Museum** ❹ (980 MacArthur Causeway; tel: 305-373-5437; www.miamichildrensmuseum.org; daily 10am–6pm; charge). Little ones can explore its range of exciting and educational interactive zones: a construction zone, an art area, a music-making studio and, this being Miami, there's also a cruise ship to play in.

Across the Causeway, children will also enjoy **Jungle Island** ❺ (1111 Parrot Jungle Trail; tel: 305-400-7000; www.jungleisland.com; daily 10am–5pm; charge), a zoological park with a petting zoo, an Everglades habitat, and a play area.

Continue along the Causeway towards Miami Beach. You'll soon reach **Palm Island**, another glitzy enclave that was once the playground of one Al Capone. Ahead is **Hibiscus Island**, an equally desirable address. Cycle back across Palm Island towards Miami Beach, with a short diversion to **Star Island**, the next left, where Miami legends Don Johnson and Gloria Estefan have both had homes.

MIAMI BEACH

Go back to the Causeway all the way back to Miami Beach proper, where you take a sharp right to follow the water around to the **Miami Beach Marina** ❻ (300 Alton Road; tel: 305-673-6000; www.miamibeachmarina.com). There's not much

to see here other than enjoy the setting and the boats, although there are shops and **Monty's on South Beach**, see ❷. There's also a deli where you can stock up if you want to have a picnic at **South Pointe Pier**. Time it right and you can get a great sunset here. To round off the route with a good meal, head back north to **Smith and Wollensky**, see ❸.

Food and Drink

❶ STK SOUTH BEACH

2305 Collins Avenue; tel: 305-604-6988; http://togrp.com/venue/stk-miami; daily D; $$$$
Stylish and sexy, this place obviously favors steak-lovers, but there are also oysters, tuna, salmon, and a daily fish special too.

❷ MONTY'S ON SOUTH BEACH

300 Alton Road; tel: 305-672-1148; www.montyssobe.com; daily L and D; $$$
This lively place near the tip of South Beach has DJs and live music and a choice of seafood dishes from the catch of the day to fish and chips, steaks, and club sandwiches.

❸ SMITH AND WOLLENSKY

1 Washington Avenue; tel: 305-673-2800; www.smithandwollensky.com/our-restaurants/miami-beach; daily L and D; $$$$
Ask for a table by the water for a view of the Miami skyline. This swanky place is all about steaks, although they do offer some seafood dishes too.

MoCA is known for its fresh approach to contemporary art

NORTH MIAMI

North Miami is a part of the city fewer visitors go, which is a shame as it has some good museums, lovely parks, historic buildings (including a unique monastery) and is great for shopping for antiques.

DISTANCE: 7 miles (11.3km)
TIME: A half day
START: Museum of Contemporary Art
END: Oleta River State Park
POINTS TO NOTE: There are some long stretches of walking so wear comfortable shoes and take plenty of water. The walk ends in a beautiful state park so set off early if you want to spend time there. To take public transportation to the start of the route, buses 10, 16 and G stop outside the Museum of Contemporary Art, while buses 9 and 75 stop a few minutes' walk away. It's also possible to get the bus back from near the end of the route. Avoid this route on a Monday, when both the Arch Creek Park and the Museum of Contemporary Art are closed (the park is also closed on Tuesdays). The Ancient Spanish Monastery sometimes closes for special events so phone or check the website first as it's a bit of a walk to get to. The Oleta River State Park has some of the best bike trails in Miami so you can rent a bike inside and there's also a big beach so take your swimming gear.

North Miami is a separate city located about 10 miles (16.1km) north of Downtown Miami, and although they merge now into one large conurbation, the history of North Miami is quite distinct. It was only incorporated as a town in 1926, known as Miami Shores. The name North Miami was adopted in 1952, when many Haitians settled here, just as Cubans did in Miami, bringing the name Little Haiti to one part of the city. It remains to this day, just like Miami, a very cosmopolitan mix of people and sights.

MUSEUM OF CONTEMPORARY ART

The route starts at the **Museum of Contemporary Art, North Miami ❶** (770 NE 125th Street; tel: 305-893-6211; http://mocanomi.org; Tue–Fri and Sun 11am–5pm, Sat 1–9pm; charge). North Miami's main art museum has an international collection of modern art, especially good for Caribbean artists and video installations. Its permanent displays are enhanced by regular changing exhibitions too.

Arch Creek Park, an old Tequesta Indian settlement

DOWN THE RABBIT HOLE

Almost opposite the museum on the far side of the street is must-see store **The Rabbit Hole** (791 NE 125th Street; tel: 305-892-0213; www.shoprabbithole.com; Tue–Sat noon–8pm, Sun 2–6pm). It specialises in vintage clothing, and the wealth of clothes on show gives the impression of browsing in a fashion museum. It does have modern clothing too, as well as jewelry – and check out the colorful bow ties!

In fact the whole of this stretch of NE 125th Street is known as Antique Row, so you can walk as far as you like in either direction, depending on how much interest you have in shopping for antiques. One shop worth seeking out is Gary Rubinstein Antiques (859 NE 125th Street; tel: 305-891-7580; http://gary rubinsteinantiques.com), east of The Rabbit Hole, on the same side of the street. There's a wide-ranging collection to be found here, from chic modern ceramics to period furniture, and while you might not have room in your suitcase to take home a stylish Italian sofa, you might be tempted by some of the smaller items, like jewelry and bowls.

Walk back towards The Rabbit Hole but before you get there turn right to walk north on NE 8th Avenue. Cross over the W. Dixie Highway. If you're hungry turn left and walk south to **Captain Jim's Seafood Market**, see ❶. Otherwise turn right to walk north along the highway. On your left you'll soon come across the **Ballet Flamenco La Rosa** (74 NE 150th Street; tel: 305-320-6982; http://ballet flamencolarosa.com, one of the US's leading flamenco companies. Check their program online in case you can come back in the evening, and they also do dance and guitar classes too.

THE PARKS

Continue walking north along the highway and for an authentic local eating experience call in at **El Kiosko Latin Café**, see ❷. Once satiated, keep walking north and at the

Miami Auto Museum classics

junction with NE 135th Street turn right to head east. After a few blocks, on the left you'll come to the beautifully named **Enchanted Forest Elaine Gordon Park** ❷ (1725 NE 135th Street; tel: 305-895-1119; daily 6am–6pm), where you can take a break from the city streets and enjoy the hiking trails, relax under the trees or maybe even take a pony ride.

Immediately east is another park, the **Arch Creek Park** (1855 NE 135th Street; tel: 305-944-6111; Wed–Sun 9am–5pm), where you can continue to enjoy the countryside in the city. A small but delightful museum and nature center here explains how this park was a Tequesta Indian settlement, making it one of the earliest settled places in Florida. Another highlight is the natural stone bridge that gives the park its name.

Miami Auto Museum

Leave the park and if you are feeling peckish head east to cross Biscayne Boulevard. In the small Keystone Plaza shopping mall on the left are a number of eating options, including **Ceviche and Grille**, see ❸. Otherwise walk north on Biscayne Boulevard for several blocks to NE 146th Street. Turn left down here and on your left is the **Miami Auto Museum** ❸ (North Building, 2000 NE 146th Street; tel: 305-354-7680; www.dezercollection.com; daily 10am–6pm; charge). The entrance fee is high but car enthusiasts will have a blast here. The collection is vast so make sure to allow plenty of time for the visit. There

are two buildings, which can be visited separately: the Classic Building, with its dazzling American Classics collection, and the Hollywood Building, which has a Batman and a James Bond exhibition on top of everything else.

SPANISH MONASTERY

On leaving the museum return to Biscayne Boulevard and continue north. It's a bit of a stretch to the next stop on this route but totally worth it. When you reach NE 163rd Street, turn left and walk west for one block. You're now back at the W. Dixie Highway, where you turn right and walk north. After crossing the river follow the highway to the right and on your right is a truly unique attraction, the remarkable **Ancient Spanish Monastery** ❹

Bike trail in Oleta River State Park

Spanish Monastery cloister   *Oleta River State Park beach*

(16711 W. Dixie Highway; tel: 305-945-1461; www.spanishmonastery.com; Mon–Sat 10am–4.30pm, Sun 11am–4.30pm, last admissions 4pm).

The Monastery of St. Bernard de Clairvaux dates back to 1133 in Northern Spain. After a revolution in the 1830s the cloisters were sold and turned into a stable. In 1925 the media magnate William Randolph Hearst bought them, along with the monastery's outbuildings, and had them dismantled and shipped to the US. Unfortunately he was struck with financial problems and the stones remained in storage in Brooklyn till the 1950s when they were bought as a tourist attraction and rebuilt, stone by stone. Later they were given to the Bishop of Florida and returned to religious use.

OLETA STATE PARK

On leaving the monastery retrace your steps south along the W. Dixie Highway, east on NE 163rd and south on Biscayne Boulevard. When you get to NE 151st Street turn left to walk east along it. After passing the athletics stadium, on your left after a few minutes you'll see the entrance to the **Oleta River State Park ❺** (3400 NE 163rd Street; tel: 305-919-1846; www.floridastateparks.org/park/Oleta-River; daily 8am–8pm; charge). This is the largest urban park in Florida and you'll want to give it as much time as you can spare. It has numerous hiking and cycling trails (you can rent bikes too), a stretch of mangrove forest, canoeing and kayaking facilities, and even a beach where you can soak your feet after the long walk.

Food and Drink

❶ CAPTAIN JIM'S SEAFOOD MARKET AND RESTAURANT

12950 W. Dixie Highway; tel: 305-892-2812; http://captainjimsmiami.com; daily L and D; $$

If you like seafood you won't get it fresher than in this casual restaurant/fish shop, where the owners buy as much as possible fresh from the boat. You can have a lighter option like a snapper sandwich or full meals.

❷ EL KIOSKO LATIN CAFÉ

13290 W. Dixie Highway; tel: 305-981-2838; www.foodxdelivery.com/restaurant/176; daily B, L and early D; $

This local favorite looks like nothing from the outside but the Caribbean food inside is good and inexpensive. Try their Puerto Rican specialty, *mofongo*, or one of their daily specials like roast goat.

❸ CEVICHE AND GRILLE

Keystone Plaza, 13521 Biscayne Blvd; tel: 305-49-0804; daily L and D; $$

In a mall full of fast-food options this casual Peruvian place stands out. Try a *ceviche mixto* plate to start, perhaps some fresh seafood Peruvian-style, and leave room for the *picarones* (donuts).

Striking art murals in Wynwood

WYNWOOD

Just north of Downtown, Wynwood is one of the most exciting areas of Miami right now, with a thriving arts scene, an alternative feel, and new bars and breweries springing up every week.

DISTANCE: 2.6 miles (4.2km)
TIME: 1 hour without stops
START: Robert Fontaine Gallery
END: Bakehouse Art Complex
POINTS TO NOTE: On the second Saturday of each month galleries stay open late, and some offer wine, food, and entertainment. Private tours are also available: https://wynwoodartwalk. com. You'll see some amazing street murals on this walk, and if this has whet your appetite for street art, you can find out more about them by taking a guided tour: www.miamisbestgraffitiguide.com. The J Wakefield Brewery offers tours on Saturdays and Sundays only, so you may want to make this a weekend visit. The Rubell Family Collection is only open Wednesday–Saturday, and the Margulies Collection is open Tuesday–Saturday.

Wynwood has seen one of the most remarkable transformations in the city. As recently as ten years ago visitors certainly had no reason to go there, and Miamians would only go if they had to.

It was a warehouse district with low appeal, even less so when the economic downturn saw the warehouses closing down. But cheap rents and empty buildings saw artists moving in, and in their wake breweries, bars, and art galleries opening up. The blank walls were transformed by colorful murals, which you'll get a chance to admire on this walk, so keeps your eyes peeled.

ART MEETS BEER

This walk starts at the **Robert Fontaine Gallery ❶** (2111 NW 2nd Avenue; tel: 305-397-8530; www.robertfontaine gallery.com; Mon–Sat noon–5pm). It may be small, with only two rooms, but what it lacks in space it makes for in quality and it's the perfect introduction to the Wynwood art scene. Regarded as one of the hippest galleries in Miami, it's also more international-thinking, and you're as likely to find Banksy here as the latest local artists.

There's another thriving art in Wynwood and that's craft brewing. Turn right out of the gallery and walk north on NW

Trendy Panther Coffee

2nd Avenue until you reach NW 24th Street. Turn right and walk east a short way, and on your right is **J Wakefield Brewing** (120 NW 24th Street; tel: 786-254-7779; www.jwakefieldbrewing.com; Tue–Thu 2–11pm, Fri–Sat noon–1am, Sun noon–8pm, Mon 2–8pm). You can't miss it because of the murals and graffiti all over it, although that applies to lots of places in Wynwood to be fair. In its tasting room you can sample some of their unique and experimental beers, like a Dragonfruit Passionfruit Florida Weisse or a Hops 4 Teacher IPA. The artsy feel continues inside too, with a giant Star Wars mural and chandeliers made from recycled wine barrels. This is definitely craft brewery meets art, and fits Wynwood to a tee.

Turn left out of the brewery to return to NW 2nd Avenue and facing you, set back from the road, is **Panther Coffee**, see ❶. If you don't want a coffee but do want more beer, turn right and immediately left along NW 24th Street. A short way along on the right is the **Concrete Beach Brewery** (325 NW 24th Street; tel: 305-796-2727; http://concrete beachbrewery.com; Mon–Tue 5–11pm, Wed–Thu and Sun noon–11pm, Fri–Sat noon–1am). Concrete Beach is a great example of how to jazz up a bland industrial space, with more art and murals and a stylish bar area with outdoor seating. There are free daily tours (Mon–Fri 6pm, Sat–Sun 1, 2, 3, 4pm), and you'll try beers with exotic names such as Tropic of Passion (a passion fruit wheat ale) and TangeR-ica (a tangerine IPA).

Turn right out of the brewery and continue west along NW 24th Street and almost at the end of the street on the right is the **Wynwood Brewing Company** (565 NW 24th Street; tel: 305-

Bright and bold Wynwood Walls

982-8732; http://wynwoodbrewing. com; Tue–Sat noon–midnight, Sun– Mon noon–10pm). This is the third (and final) brewery on the tour, but the breweries are very much part of what Wynwood is about, and the Wynwood Brewing Company also has its share of murals and other artworks for you to enjoy, whether you stop for a beer or not. There are brewery tours at weekends (2pm and 6pm; charge), a tap room with happy hours (Mon–Fri 4–7pm), food trucks on Fridays and, on the second Saturday of every month, a pop-up art gallery.

WYNWOOD WALLS

When you leave the brewery turn left and walk all the way back to NW 2nd Avenue. Turn left to walk north along here and on your left is the entrance to the **Wynwood Walls** ❷ (2520 NW 2nd Avenue; tel: 305-531-4411; www.thewynwoodwalls. com; Mon–Thu 10.30am–11.30pm, Fri– Sat 10.30am–midnight, Sun 10.30am– 8pm; free). This remarkable outdoor art project encapsulates the Wynwood spirit; it consists of walls that have been vibrantly painted by graffiti and street artists from all over the world. There's also a shop where you can buy original artworks.

Turn left when you leave the Wynwood Walls, then left again on NW 26th Street and on your right is **Walt Grace Vintage** (229 NW 26th Street; tel: 786-483-8180; www.waltgracevintage.com; Tue–Fri 10am–7pm, Sat 10am–5pm,

Sun noon–5pm). A shop, museum and gallery all-in-one, this is not where art meets ale for a change but where art meets cars and guitars. Collections of vintage cars and guitars are on display alongside walls covered in artworks. Some are for sale and some are for show, including a Volkswagen Beetle once owned by Jerry Seinfeld.

If you want a pastry, snack or coffee, turn left when you leave for **Zak the Baker DELI**, see ❷. Otherwise return to NW 2nd Avenue and walk north a few blocks up. Just before you hit NW 29th Street is the **Boxelder Craft Beer Market**, see ❸. Turn right, and a few minutes' walk east, on your right, stands the **O Cinema** (90 NW 29th Street; tel: 305-571-9970; www.o-cinema.org/venue/o-cinema-wynwood). More than a mere cinema, it's a cultural reference point for the revival of the Wynwood neighborhood. It was just another empty warehouse until the small Miami O Cinema chain converted it as an independent arthouse cinema in 2011. It has only one screen, with four shows a day – morning, noon, evening and late-night – and if the timing is right it's worth ducking in here for a show, one that you will share with just 111 other people.

TWO COLLECTIONS

Directly opposite the cinema is the **Rubell Family Collection** ❸ (95 NW 29th Street; tel: 305-573-6090; https://rfc.museum; Wed–Sat 10am–

Rubell Family Collection   *Gallery at the Bakehouse Art Complex*

5.30pm; charge). This contemporary arts foundation is housed in yet another former warehouse, though it's hard to tell from the outside after the make-over it was given. Inside is one of the largest privately-owned collections of contemporary art in the world, first established in New York City in 1964 by Donald and Mera Rubell and now amounting to over 7,300 works. There are also visiting exhibitions. Note that the gallery will be relocating in 2018 to a new purpose-built building in the Allapattah district, to the west of Wynwood.

On leaving, turn right and walk west back along NW 29th Street to NW 5th Avenue. Turn left here and go south down the avenue unyil NW 27th Street, and turn right. At the end of the street on the right is **The Margulies Collection at the WAREhOUSE ❹** (591 NW 27th Street; tel: 305-576-1051; www.margulies warehouse.com; Tue–Sat 11am–4pm; charge), another warehouse that has been converted into a huge and airy space to house this collection of contemporary art, photography, video, sculpture, and various installations.

On leaving, turn right and right again to walk north up NW 6th Avenue and at the junction with NW 32nd Street is the **Bakehouse Art Complex** (561 NW 32nd Street; tel: 305-576-2828; www.bacfl. org; daily noon–5pm; free). By way of a change this is not a former warehouse but instead an arts center housed in a former Art Deco bakery building. There are changing exhibitions, artists in residence, classes, and lots of events happening, so check the program first and see what's taking place to time your visit.

Food and Drink

❶ PANTHER COFFEE
2390 NW 2nd Avenue; tel: 305-677-3952; www.panthercoffee.com; Mon–Sat 7am–9pm, Sun 7am–8pm; $
This ultra-hip coffee shop fits in perfectly with the Wynwood vibe, and you'll often find arts or music events taking place. If you like their slow-roasted coffee you can buy beans to take away too.

❷ ZAK THE BAKER DELI
405 NW 26th Street; tel: 786-347-7100; https://zakthebaker.com; Sun–Thu 8am–5pm, Fri 8am–2.30pm; $$
If you want a quick snack and a coffee, this kosher bakery serves food and has a deli counter too. A relaxed approach means that both breakfast and lunch are available all day. Try the corned beef hash.

❸ BOXELDER CRAFT BEER MARKET
2817 NW 2nd Avenue; tel: 305-942-7769; www.bxldr.com; Mon 4pm–midnight, Tue–Thu 1pm–midnight, Fri–Sat 1pm–2am, Sun 1–10pm; $
Breweries naturally sell their own beers but this beer-tap-cum-bottle-shop has a head-spinning range of local brews for you to try. Special events showcase specific breweries.

Jewish tombs at the Miami City Cemetery

OVERTOWN

Historically Miami's black neighborhood, Overtown today is an exciting and diverse area of museums, parks, community gardens, and historic buildings, especially churches – all a testament to the fascinating story of this special place in Miami's history.

> **DISTANCE:** 2.5 miles (4km)
> **TIME:** 1 hour without stops
> **START:** City of Miami Cemetery
> **END:** Lyric Theater
> **POINTS TO NOTE:** The Historic Black Police Precinct Courthouse and Museum is closed Sundays and Mondays. Overtown is easily accessible by Metrorail.

Northwest of Downtown, Overtown is a mainly black neighborhood. Once referred to as 'Colored Town', the city's race relations – good and bad – are illustrated in the churches, museums and archives of today. Because Miami has been mostly associated with Cuban migrants, the story of black Miami is less well-known than in other southern cities, and while that story isn't as dramatic as, say, Birmingham's or Memphis's, it's still a story that needs telling.

CITY OF MIAMI CEMETERY

This route starts at the **City of Miami Cemetery** ❶ (1800 NE 2nd Avenue; tel: 305-579-6938; www.miamigov.com/parks/cemetery.html). Located between Downtown and Overtown, this is the city's oldest cemetery, dating back to 1887, just a year after the city was incorporated. Julia Tuttle, known as the Mother of Miami (see page 11) is buried here, along with many other prominent citizens. In 1989 it was placed on the US National Register of Historic Places.

There are thousands of people buried here and, as with cemeteries everywhere, the history of the place reflects the history of the area. When it was first opened, it was a segregated cemetery, with separate areas for blacks and whites. Later a Jewish area was added. Here too are buried the fallen heroes of various wars, including the Civil War, the Spanish-American War, and the two World Wars. Today only about 1,000 burial plots remain, so the criteria for securing one are very strict.

PARKS

Leave the cemetery by the main entrance and turn right to walk west on NE 17th Terrace. At the end of the street turn right

Children playing football in Dorsey Park

for one block, then turn left heading west on NW 19th Street. At the junction with NW 1st Avenue turn right and walk south. On your left is **Dorsey Park** (1701 NW 1st Avenue; tel: 305-579-6940; www.miamigov.com/parks/park_dorsey.html; daily 9am–8pm). This small park with a children's play area and sports facilities is named after Dana A. Dorsey. Born in 1872, Dorsey became one of Miami's early successful black businessmen, and one of the first black millionaires in the southern US. He owned the Dorsey Hotel, the first black-owned hotel in Miami, and he opened a bank for the city's black citizens. He also donated land for the building of schools, and his other philanthropic acts included providing the land for this park for the use of black Miamians.

On leaving the park, head south. If it's coffee time, turn left on NW 17th Street and right on N Miami Avenue for **Vice City Bean**, see ❶. Continue south down NW 1st Avenue for a few blocks until NW 12th Street, where you turn right and walk west. At the end is the much larger **Gibson Park** (401 NW 12th Street; tel: 305-960-4646; www.miamigov.com/parks/park_gibson.html; daily 7am–9pm), a pleasant place to stroll, and there are lots of fun kids' activities, football and baseball grounds, and a pool (Mon–Fri 1–7pm, Sat noon–5pm).

BLACK HISTORY

Historic Black Police Precinct Courthouse and Museum

From the park, walk back to NW 3rd Avenue and turn right to walk south. Turn right on NW 11th Street until you reach, on your left, the **Historic Black Police Precinct Courthouse and Museum** ❷ (480 NW 11th Street; tel: 305-329-2513; http://historicalblackprecinct.org; Tue–Sat 10am–4pm; charge). Built in 1950 when the south was still segregated, this was the headquarters for the city's black police officers and one black judge, who were tasked with fighting crime in their local, mostly black community. They were

Mt. Zion Baptist Church

under the authority of a white Police Captain and three white Lieutenants. It was a tough time, as the officers found themselves not only dealing with the problems of black crime, but also the prejudices of the rest of the white police force in Miami. They did start to bring some sense of law and order to what was then called the 'Colored Precinct', and their story is sympathetically told here. The precinct was disbanded in 1963 and its 79 black officers absorbed into the rest of the police force.

Mt. Zion Baptist Church

Walk back east along NW 11th Street and turn right onto NW 3rd Avenue. If you're hungry then **House of Wings**, see ❷, is a good option or a little further on the right is **Jackson Soul Food**, see ❸. A few steps away is the **Mt. Zion Baptist Church** (301 NW 9th Street; tel: 305-379-4147), founded in 1896 by Dana A. Dorsey and a group of others. It was one of the main places in Miami for blacks to meet during the struggles for Civil Rights, and Dr Martin Luther King Jnr came here. It's still in use as an active church, with one of the oldest black congregations in Miami. In 1988 it was placed on the US National Register of Historic Places.

Historic Ward Rooming House

Leave the church and turn left to head east on NW 9th Street. On your left here the **Historic Ward Rooming House** (249 NW 9th Street; tel: 786-439-9718) was built in 1925 to provide lodgings and a safe haven not just for blacks but for Native Americans who needed somewhere to stay for the night. Inside is a gallery and exhibition space, and there are regular artistic events. Although it was only an ordinary rooming house, it's significant because not many buildings from that time still stand.

Dana A. Dorsey House

Opposite is the **Dana A. Dorsey House** (250 NW 9th Street), the comparatively modest home of black millionaire Dana A. Dorsey. Built in 1913, it was placed on the National Register of Historic Places in 1989 and reconstructed in 1995. It is now owned by the Black Archives History and Research Foundation of South Florida, who use it as social services offices, and it cannot be visited.

Continue east along NW 9th Street to reach the start of the **Ninth Street Pedestrian Mall** ❸ – not a shopping mall but a very pleasant long, thin park popular for festivals and general get-togethers. The striking lamp-posts and main square showcase the colors of Africa, to celebrate the neighborhood's African-American heritage. Other parts of the park were inspired by African textile weavings.

Greater Bethel African Methodist Episcopal Church

Go back to the start of the mall and turn left to walk south on NW 2nd Avenue, passing the Lyric Theater which we'll return to. Turn right on NW 8th Street and on the right is the **Greater Bethel African Methodist Episcopal Church** (245 NW 8th Street;

Historic Lyric Theater

tel: 305-371-9102; call for opening hours), another of Overtown's significant historic churches. The first church on the site was built in 1896 before the city of Miami was even incorporated, making this one of the oldest church congregations in the city. Work on the present church began in 1927 in the Mediterranean Revival style. However, funds were raised by the congregation as and when they could, and building wasn't completed until 1943. In 1958 Dr Martin Luther King Jnr delivered a speech here, and it was listed in the National Register of Historic Places in 1992. It is still an active church but isn't always open to visitors so call ahead.

The Black Archives

Retrace your steps to the **Lyric Theater/ Black Archives** ❹ (819 NW 2nd Avenue; tel: 786-708-4610; www.bahlt.org). This whole area was once a thriving theater and nightlife area, earning the nickname of Little Broadway, but the Lyric Theater, which opened in 1913, is the only building that survives from that era. It then became a movie theater and a venue for touring musicians; Aretha Franklin, Count Basie, Sam Cooke, B.B. King and Ella Fitzgerald have all played here. Now a venue for music, drama, exhibitions, and special events, it's well worth trying to catch a show in its intimate 400-seater theater.

The theater has another significant role as the home for the Black Archives History and Research Foundation of South Florida to give it its full title, the organisation which now owns the Lyric. This archive docu-

ments the African-American experience in the whole of southern Florida, not just Overtown, but the archive is naturally very involved in what goes on here. Don't miss the chance to visit this special venue, and see the current displays and exhibitions.

Food and Drink

❶ VICE CITY BEAN

1657 N Miami Avenue; tel: 305-726-8031; http://vicecitybean.com; daily 7am–7pm; $

One of the city's best coffee shops, it also serve pastries and baked treats, but the focus is on making the best coffee around.

❷ HOUSE OF WINGS

1039 NW 3rd Avenue; tel: 305-371-6556; www.houseofwingsmiami.com; Mon–Thu 11am–8pm, Fri–Sat 11am–9pm, Sun 11am–7pm; $$

This simple place gives you a real taste of the South, and they serve the best wings in Overtown. Also try their lemon pepper chicken with yellow rice, or conch salad, and leave some space for the home-made cakes.

❸ JACKSON SOUL FOOD

950 NW 3rd Avenue; tel: 305-374-7661; www.jacksonsoulfood.com; Mon–Wed 6am–2pm, Thu–Sun 6am–7pm; $$

You have to eat soul food while you're in Overtown and this unassuming neighborhood place will have you talking to your fellow diners while tucking into BBQ ribs, pork chops, catfish, or other southern favorites.

Calle Ocho, the pulsing hub of Little Havana

LITTLE HAVANA

In Little Havana, Latin traditions linger longest, a neighborhood where not only Cubans but immigrants from the Caribbean and Central America have made Miami their home. This is one of the city's most vibrant areas, a constantly changing assertion of new beginnings and hope.

DISTANCE: 1.5 miles (2.4km)
TIME: 30 minutes without stops
START: Bay of Pigs Museum and Library
END: Cuban Memorial Plaza
POINTS TO NOTE: Be sensitive before making political comments about relationships between Cuba and the US as some people here have extreme views. Try to come here on the last Friday of the month to round off the evening with live music at the Viernes Culturales (Cultural Fridays). On the second Friday of the month there's Little Havana Art Walk, when galleries stay open late and there's a chance to meet the artists. If visiting in March the annual Carnaval Calle Ocho Festival (see page 111) is a highlight. The Bay of Pigs Museum is closed at weekends, but don't let that deter you from coming here to soak in the fun of a Saturday night in Little Havana.

You could say that if you haven't seen Little Havana, you haven't seen Miami. This is especially true now, with the death of Fidel Castro and a thawing of relationships between the US and Cuba. This may of course change in the future, but either way things are definitely happening between the two countries, and you'll get no closer take on it than in Little Havana. The area earned its nickname in the 1960s, after there was an increasing influx of immigrants from Cuba during the political turmoil of the 1950s, especially after the Cuban Revolution of 1959 overthrew the government and set up a communist state. Many people fled, both the wealthy and the poor, and a lot settled in this corner of Miami.

Little Havana isn't solely a Cuban enclave, though, as it's also home to immigrants from other Latin American countries, throwing their culture into the mix. Of course you don't have to be interested in history or politics to enjoy your time here, as it's simply a fun neighborhood with colorful traditions, galleries, parks, cigar factories, great shopping, and tasty Cuban food. Simply walking along the main street, Calle Ocho, smelling the Cuban food and coffee to the beat of salsa music wafting out of doorways, creates a general feel-good atmosphere.

The Bay of Pigs Museum honors the men who died during the ill-fated invasion

BAY OF PIGS MUSEUM

The first stop, if you want to learn more about Cuban history, is the **Bay of Pigs Museum ❶** (1821 SW 9th Street; tel: 305-649-4719; www.bayofpigs2506.com; Mon–Fri 9am–4pm; charge). This small museum also goes by the name of the Brigade 2506 Museum and Library, after the group of exiles in Miami who were sent by the CIA to help a planned invasion of Cuba (see box page 56). The brigade suffered many casualties at the Bay of Pigs, and the museum includes the brigade flag that was held by President Kennedy when he welcomed the survivors back to Miami. From one angle the Bay of Pigs story was a humiliating fiasco for the US, but from some Cuban perspectives it was a heroic attempt to take back their island from Fidel Castro's illegal government, through which some people lost their lives. When in Little Havana it's best to see things from all perspectives.

CALLE OCHO

Art galleries

Turn left out of the museum to walk east on SW 9th Street, then left on SW 17th Avenue and right on SW 8th Street, known locally as Calle Ocho (8th Street) and the main drag for Little Havana. A short way along on your right is the **Agustin Gainza Arts and Tavern** (1652 SW 8th Street; tel: 305-644-5855; www.agustingainza.com; Tue–Fri 11am–6pm, Sat noon–4pm, Sun–Mon by appointment only), a wonderful combination of art gallery and café-bar. Here you can have a glass of wine, a beer or a mojito while enjoying the work of the artist-owner, Agustin Gainza, a multi-media Cuban-American artist who seems equally adept whether painting, sculpting, or making ceramics.

Further along is **Cremata Fine Art** (1646 SW 8th Street; tel: 305-644-3315/ 305-300-0068; www.crematafineart.com; Tue–Sat noon–7pm). This gallery run by artist, activist and art collector Raul Cremata displays and sells boldly-colored paintings, sculptures, and prints of Cuban and other Latin American artists, with a monthly solo exhibition too.

Further along still is the **Molina Fine Art Gallery** (1634 SW 8th Street; tel: 305-642-0444; www.molinaartgallery.com; Mon–Sat 11am–7pm).

Map labels: SW 5th Street, SW 17th Ave, SW 16th Ave, LITTLE HAVANA, SW 6th Street, SW 6th Street, Little Havana Cigar Factory, Cubaocho Museum & Performing Arts Center, Calle 8 Cigars, Futurama Building, SW 7th Street, Agustin Gainza Arts And Tavern ❷, Calle Ocho Walk of Fame, SW 8th St, SW 8th Street, SW 12th Ave, Cremata Fine Art LLC, Molina Art Gallery Inc, Maximo Gomez Park ❸ ❹ ❶, Little Havana Visitor Center, La Tradicion Cubana Inc, SW 9th St, ❶ Bay of Pigs Museum & Library, Tower Theater, SW 10th Street, SW 13th Ave, SW 18th Ave, SW 11th Street, SW 16th Ave, SW 15th Ave, SW 14th Ave, SW 13th Ct, SW 12th Ave, SW 12th Ct, N, SW 11th Terrace, SW 14th Ave, SW 13th Ct, Cuban Memorial Boulevard Park ❺, 300 m / 330 yds, SW 12th Street

The inviting Azucar Ice Cream Company

Luis Molina was born in Cuba and studied art at the National School of Design in Havana before moving to and exhibiting widely in the United States. He combines his Cuban roots with a fascination for Africa, and his paintings are sometimes spiritual, sometimes erotic – and sometimes both at the same time.

The Bay of Pigs

Following the Cuban Revolution of 1959, leader Fidel Castro turned Cuba into a communist state with increasingly close ties with the then USSR, the US's Cold War foe. The US was worried by these changes in an island just 130 miles (209km) from the Florida coast. A group of Cuban military refugees in Miami, who had fled Cuba after the revolution, volunteered to go back and try to defeat Castro, with the help of the CIA and the approval of President Eisenhower, who provided them with $13 million. About 1,300 men took off in separate forces from both Nicaragua and Guatemala and, aided by paratroopers, landed at the Bay of Pigs on the south coast of Cuba. Within three days, 114 of them were dead and the rest captured by the Cubans. It cost the US a further $53 million in aid to secure their release. They were greeted back on American soil by President Kennedy at the Orange Bowl in Miami, and some of the survivors went on to form the Brigade 2506 Veteran's Association, which runs the Bay of Pigs Museum in Little Havana.

On the north side of Calle Ocho from these galleries is **Futurama 1637 ②** (1637 SW 8th Street; tel: 305-643-5500; Mon–Fri 10am–6pm), an art space established in 2011 to provide working studios and gallery space for twelve resident artists. They also have occasional events, including live music.

Little Havana Cigar Factory
Continue east along Calle Ocho and, on the south side just after SW 16th Avenue, is **El Pub**, see ①, a good spot for a Cuban bite to eat. Opposite El Pub on the north side of the street, is another good option, **El Cristo**, see ②. Otherwise continue east and further along on the north side you'll find the **Little Havana Cigar Factory** (1501 SW 8th Street; tel: 305-541-1103; www.littlehavanacigarstore.com; Tue–Sat 10am–7pm, Sun–Mon 10am–6pm). There are many cigar shops and factories in Little Havana. Due to the trade embargo between the US and Cuba it is not possible to buy Cuban cigars in the US so what is on offer here are Cuban-style cigars made in Miami, often with displays of how to make a cigar. This is one of the more upmarket outlets which stocks a wide range of cigars and other accessories, and also has a smoking room.

Next to the Cigar factory is **Ball and Chain**, see ③, if you're feeling peckish. If it's a refreshing ice-cream you're after on the other hand head to the **Azucar Ice Cream Company**, see ④.

The Cigar Factory's finest   *A game of dominoes in the eponymous park*

Tower Theater

Opposite, on the south side of Calle Ocho, stands a Little Havana icon, the **Tower Theater** ❸ (1508 SW 8th Street; tel: 305-643-8706; www.towertheatermiami.com; see website for show times). This movie theater opened in 1926, when it was the finest state-of-the-art cinema in the southern US, and it remains one of the oldest cultural buildings in Miami. A few years later it was given an Art Deco exterior and its trademark steel tower. It's been a central part of the lives of Cuban immigrants, serving to introduce them to American culture and to keep them in touch with their own. After a lengthy period of closure, today it's thriving again as both a movie theater and a local cultural center.

Domino Park

On the far side of SW 15th Avenue from the theater is another local landmark, **Maximo Gomez Park (Domino Park)** ❹ (801 SW 15th Avenue; tel: 305-859-2717; daily 9am–6pm), named after the Cuban Major-General in their war against Spain (1868–78). Nicknamed Domino Park, local residents, mostly Cuban-American men, come here to enjoy a game of dominoes and chew the fat.

East of the park on Calle Ocho is the **Little Havana Visitor Center** (1442 SW 8th Street; tel: 305-643-5500; Tue–Wed 11am–4pm). This is a fairly new initiative and at the time of writing was only open two days a week for limited hours.

Opposite the center, on the north side of Calle Ocho, is the **Cubaocho**

Museum and Performing Arts Center

(1465 SW 8th Street #106; tel: 305-285-5880; www.cubaocho.com; Wed, Fri–Sat 11am–3am, Tue 11am–10pm, Thu 11am–11pm, Sun–Mon closed; free). Set up by a Cuban who escaped to the US in a boat in 1992, it's an unusual blend of museum, art gallery, music and dance venue, party space with a rum bar thrown in for good measure.

Walk of Fame

Along Calle Ocho between SW 12th Avenue and SW 17th Avenue stretches the **Calle Ocho Walk of Fame**, also called the Latin Walk of Fame. The pink marble stars on the sidewalk look just like their Hollywood counterparts, but these honor figures from Cuba and other Latin American cultures. There has been some controversy: some feel it should feature only people of Cuban descent. There were demonstrations in 1989 when the Spanish singer Raphael got a star, as he was the first non-Cuban to be honoured. Other stars to look for include Gloria Estefan, Enrique Iglesias, boxer Roberto Duran, and Cuban singer and dancer Celia Cruz, known as the Queen of Salsa.

Strolling along the Walk look on the south side of Calle Ocho for **La Tradición Cubana Cigars** (1336 SW 8th Street; tel: 305-643-4005; www.tradicion.com; Mon-Fri 10am–5pm, Sat 10am–3pm). This cigar factory and shop was founded in 1995 but since the factory burned down in 2006, their cigars have been made in the Dominican Republic using a blend

A patriotic mural

of Dominican, Nicaraguan, Ecuadorian, Brazilian, and Honduran tobacco, aged in Spanish cedar wood. For more cigars, continue walking east on the north side of Calle Ocho till you get to **Calle 8 Cigars** (1221 SW 8th Street; tel: 305-285-1244; Mon–Sat 10am–9pm, Sun 10am–6pm). This small and modest store has a good range of cigars from around the world, and with attractive prices.

CUBAN MEMORIAL PLAZA

Walk back west on Calle Ocho on the south side, until you reach the corner with SW 13th Avenue and the **Cuban Memorial Plaza ❺**. There's quite a lot to see on the plaza: a monument to the Bay of Pigs invasion, a statue of the Virgin Mary, a map of the island of Cuba and a bust of José Martí, the author who became a Cuban national hero. The sense of Cuban pride and identity is palpable and, unsurprisingly, it's a popular rallying spot for meetings and demonstrations. To leave the bustle of Calle Ocho, walk south along the tree-lined street, officially SW 13th Avenue but also called Cuban Memorial Boulevard, and foray into the residential parts of Little Havana.

Food and Drink

❶ EL PUB

1548 SW 8th Street; tel: 305-642-9942; http://elpubrestaurant.com; Sun–Thu 7am–11pm, Fri–Sat 7am–midnight; $$
This busy and colorful place offers an authentic Cuban dining experience. Choose from a simple Cuban sandwich or a *bocadito*, or go for a fuller meal of smoked pork chops or the Pub's specialty, *parrillada* (a Cuban mixed grill).

❷ EL CRISTO

1543 SW 8th Street; tel: 305-643-9992; www.elcristorestaurant.com; Mon–Thu 8am–10pm, Fri–Sun 8am–11pm; $$
This casual Cuban restaurant in business since 1972 serves specialties like *boliche* (beef pot roast) or *lechón asado* (pulled pork with grilled onions).

❸ BALL AND CHAIN

1513 SW 8th Street; tel: 305-643-7820; https://ballandchainmiami.com; Mon–Wed noon–midnight, Thu–Sat noon–3am, Sun 2–10pm; $$$
This iconic place opened as a nightclub in the 1930s and today is more of a live music venue with tables for dinner. You'll need to book for dinner but stop by for a lunch of *chicharrón* or a roasted pork taco.

❹ AZUCAR ICE CREAM COMPANY

1503 SW 8th Street; tel: 305-381-0369; www.azucaricecream.com; Mon–Wed 11am–9pm, Thu–Sat 11am–11pm, Sun 11am–10pm; $
The owner's Cuban grandmother had a passion for ice-cream and the amazing flavors here are inspired by Florida's climate and tropical fruits. Don't dismiss it as just another ice-cream parlor.

The Freedom Tower, modeled after the Giralda in Spain

DOWNTOWN MIAMI

Beneath Downtown's shiny skyscrapers are some of the oldest buildings in Miami, as well as museums, parks, churches, restaurants, galleries, and the occasional view of the harbor.

DISTANCE: 3 miles (4.8km)
TIME: 1 hour without stops
START: Freedom Tower
END: Miami Riverwalk
POINTS TO NOTE: In September the DWNTWN Art Days showcase 50 special art events, exhibitions, movies, and public projects (www.facebook.com/DWNTWNarts). If you're traveling with kids then on the second Saturday of each month, the HistoryMiami Museum organises family fun days with lots of free activities.

The downtowns in American cities can be hit or miss affairs. Some are bland business districts filled with office workers and branches of Starbucks, while others – such as in Chicago, New York, or Nashville – are all thriving places with their own distinct identities. And Miami is the latter. In fact there's so much going on in this revitalised Downtown that we have split it into three different routes: Downtown, Brickell (see page 67), and the Bay area (see page 63).

FREEDOM TOWER

Begin this route at the **Freedom Tower** ❶ (600 Biscayne Blvd; http://mdcmoad.org/freedom-tower). At 266 feet (78m), the tower is dwarfed by Downtown's skyscrapers but it matches any of them for grace and style. Built in 1925 as *The Miami News* head office, it was modelled on the bell tower of the Giralda Cathedral in Seville, Spain. When the newspaper relocated in 1957, the building was used for 12 years as a processing center for the numerous refugees who were fleeing the revolution in Castro's Cuba. It was then it got its name of Freedom Tower, but was also referred to as the 'Ellis Island of the South', in reference to New York's similar processing center for refugees and immigrants from all over the world. In 2008 the tower became a National Historic Landmark, and today it is run by Miami Dade College, who show special exhibitions there as well as having offices. On the second floor you'll also find the MDC Museum of Art and Design, although this is closed for renovation until spring 2018.

Exhibition at the HistoryMiami Museum

From the Freedom Tower turn right a short way south down Biscayne Boulevard, turn right to walk west on NE 6th Street, then left to walk south on NE 2nd Avenue. On your way, on your left, you'll come across the upscale **Tuyo Restaurant**, see ❶. When you reach NE 2nd Street turn right, and on the left is the pretty and pink **Gesu Catholic Church** (118 NE 2nd Street; tel: 305-379-1424; http://gesuchurch.org), the oldest Catholic church in southern Florida. The Mediterranean-Revival structure, built in 1921 on the site of its 1890s predecessor, is noted for its stained glass, murals and organ. It also houses the Centro Hispano Católico, which has played a huge part in welcoming and assisting Miami's Cuban and other immigrants over the years by way of food, clothing, education, and housing.

LUMMUS PARK

Continue west on NE 2nd Street, turn right on N Miami Avenue, then left on NW 3rd Street. After several blocks you will arrive in front of **Lummus Park** (404 NW 3rd Street; tel: 305-416-1416; www.miamigov.com/parks/park_lummus.html; Mon–Fri 9am–6pm; free), part of the Historic Lummus Park District covering 2.4 hectares (6 acres). The park was established in 1909 as the burgeoning city's first green space, with the area around it a new residential district. Now of course these are some of the oldest buildings in Miami, showcasing various architectural styles. Within the park are two notable historic buildings, both of which were moved here from elsewhere to preserve them. The wooden William Wagner

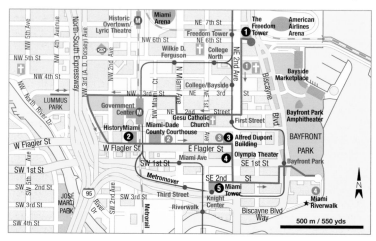

Inside the Olympia Theater

House was built in the 1850s by pioneer and settler William Wagner and his Creole wife, while Fort Dallas is an 1830s military post that stood originally by the Miami River during the Seminole Wars.

HISTORYMIAMI MUSEUM

Walk back east along NW 3rd Street then turn right to walk south down NW 3rd Avenue. This swings east and becomes W Flagler Street. After passing NW 2nd Avenue take the steps on your left up to the **HistoryMiami Museum** ➋ (101 W Flagler Street; tel: 305-375-1492; www.historymiami.org; Mon–Sat 10am–5pm, Sun noon–5pm; charge). Dating back to 1940, this is the largest history museum in Florida, with a permanent collection ranging from ancient archaeology to modern fashion. There's also an excellent Photography Center as well as changing exhibitions. The museum also arranges some of the best city tours in Miami, covering topics like crime and architecture, and with night-time walks and river and bay cruises too.

From here, return to W Flagler Street and continue east. On the left you'll soon see the impressive **Miami-Dade County Courthouse** (73 W Flagler Street: tel: 305-275-1155; www.miami-dadeclerk.com; Mon–Fri 9am–4pm). When it opened in 1925, it was the first high-rise building in the county and features in the US National Register of Historic Places. Still the county's main courthouse, you can take a look inside, but it is a working building.

A BANK AND A THEATER

Continue east along Flagler and on your left you may be tempted by **Mario the Baker Pizza**, see ➋. Or cross NE 1st Avenue, and almost at the end of the block is the stylish **Alfred I. duPont Building** ➌ (169 E Flagler Street #5; tel: 305-358-4203; www.thedupontbuilding.com). This 1939 building was originally the home of the Florida National Bank, and was named after the bank's owner. The exterior is a mix of Art Deco features and Modern architecture. The inside is even more impressive, with marble walls and floor, brass elevators and hand-painted ceilings. Its ballrooms are now used for weddings and private functions.

Opposite, the **Olympia Theater** ➍ (174 E Flagler Street; tel: 305-374-2444; www.olympiatheater.org; see page 107) was built in 1926 as a movie theater and later became a venue for variety and music shows: the Marx Brothers, Ella Fitzgerald, Elvis Presley, Pavarotti, and BB King have all performed here. It still hosts shows, music, drama, talks, comedy, both in the main theater and in the Lobby Lounge.

Turn left past the theater and north on NE 2nd Avenue is veggie-heaven **Manna Life Food**, see ➌. Or turn right past the theater and walk south down NE 2nd Avenue and at the junction with SE 1st Street is the **meetinghouse** (168 SE 1st Street; tel: 305-790-3681; www.meetinghousemiami.org; times vary). This artists' collective puts on contemporary exhibitions, sometimes controversial but never boring.

All curves – the dazzling Miami Tower and Metromover track

MIAMI TOWER

Continue south down NE 2nd Avenue and turn right on SE 2nd Street where the **Miami Tower** ❺ (100 SE 2nd Street; tel: 305-539-7100) will soon come into view. Built in 1987, this 47-floor office building is the 8th tallest building in Florida (and in Miami), scraping the sky at 625ft (191m). Ten of those floors comprise the parking garage. It's known for its night-time illumination, which changes in color and theme according to holidays and seasons.

From the junction, walk east on SE 2nd Street, turn left at the end onto S. Biscayne Blvd, then right onto SE 1st Street and cross over into the park ahead of you. Walk through the park in a southeast direction until you reach the **Miami Riverwalk**. This pedestrian walkway leads along the edge of Biscayne Bay and you can walk south where the path then goes along the north side of the Miami River. You can walk along here as far as you like, though the walk is sometimes blocked by construction work on riverfront developments, so be prepared to retrace your steps at some stage, back into the heart of downtown Miami. To round off with a meal and a water view, make your way to **Il Gabbiano**, see ❹.

Food and Drink

❶ TUYO RESTAURANT

415 NE 2nd Avenue; tel: 305-237-3200; www.tuyomiami.com; Mon–Fri L and D, Sat D; $$$$

This smart, sophisticated place specializes in contemporary American cuisine. Miami's celebrities flock here for its seared Hudson Valley foie gras and harissa-encrusted rack of lamb. There's also a six-course tasting menu with optional wine pairings.

❷ MARIO THE BAKER PIZZA

43 W Flagler Street; tel: 786-316-0166; www.ordermariothebaker.com; daily L and D; $$

Mario delivers quality pizzas at decent prices with a simple décor and a convivial atmosphere. Calzones, pastas, chicken, and meat dishes are also available.

❸ MANNA LIFE FOOD

80 NE 2nd Avenue; tel: 786-717-5060; http://mannalifefood.com; Mon–Fri L and early D, Sat L; $$

This chic place is vegetarian and gluten-free, offering friendly service and tasty dishes such as baked tofu, a southwestern 3-bean bowl and veggie pesto, or you can just get some cookies and coffee or smoothies to take away.

❹ IL GABBIANO

335 Biscayne Blvd; tel: 305-373-0063; www.ilgabbianomia.com; Mon–Fri L and D, Sat D; $$$

This smart white-tablecloth place combines superb views over the water with impressive Italian food. Its extensive menu includes pasta and risotto, and mains like veal sautéed in fresh cream and Gorgonzola cheese, or filet of beef with Barolo wine sauce.

A splash of pink: the Metromover in Downtown

THE BAY BY METROMOVER

Use Miami's public transportation system, by way of the Metrorail, Metromover and buses, and the entire city opens up to you. This short route hugs the bay, taking in several fine museums along the way.

DISTANCE: 2.5 miles (4km)
TIME: One day, allowing for museum visits and public transportation
START: Trinity Cathedral
END: Bayfront Park
POINTS TO NOTE: See page 117 for information on public transportation. The Pérez Art Museum is closed on Wednesdays but open until 9pm on Thursdays. The Science Barge is only open on Saturdays. You can combine this tour with both the Brickell (see page 67) and the Downtown routes (see page 59), as the areas overlap.

This route combines walking and Metromover to explore the east side of Downtown, close to Biscayne Bay.

TRINITY CATHEDRAL

Begin the tour at the impressive **Trinity Cathedral ❶** (464 NE 16th Street; tel: 305-374-3372; www.trinitymiami.org), ensconced amidst the Downtown skyscrapers. The original wooden church

here was founded in June 1896, a month before the city itself was incorporated, making it the oldest church in the original city limits. It was replaced by a stone church in 1912, and then in 1925 the present building opened to provide extra space for a fast-growing parish. Inside is a remarkable collection of mosaics and stained glass, the Jubilee Altar with its five crosses, and an Aeolian-Skinner organ. It's worth trying to visit during Evensong or an organ recital.

Walking west on NE 15th Street, on the south side of the cathedral, you'll soon see the elevated tracks of Miami's Metromover system. Make a left turn under the tracks when you get to N Bayshore Drive and walk south. You're actually close to the Metromover station of the **Adrienne Arsht Center for the Performing Arts ❷** (1300 Biscayne Blvd; tel: 305-949-6722; www.arshtcenter.org), which you reach by turning right on NE 14th Street and then left on Biscayne Blvd. This is the largest performing arts center in Florida (see page 107), and even if you don't plan to go to a performance, the building itself is worth a look. It opened in 2006 and two years

A fun display at the Frost Museum of Science

later acquired its name when Adrienne Arsht, a businesswoman and philanthropist, donated $30 million to ensure the center's financial survival. It's now home to the Florida Grand Opera and the Miami City Ballet and also puts on many other shows in its exquisite auditoriums.

MUSEUM PARK

Return north along N Bayshore Drive heading back towards the cathedral, but when you reach NE 15th Street turn left for the Adrienne Arsht Center Metromover station. There's only one line here so take the next train going south and get off at the next station, Museum Park.

Frost Museum of Science

Opposite the station gleams the new **Frost Museum of Science** ❸ (3280 S Miami Avenue; tel: 305-646-4200; www.frostscience.org; daily 9am–6pm; charge). Opened in 2017, having been relocated from elsewhere in the city, the museum is made up of four separate buildings. One houses the 250-seater Planetarium, one of the most advanced in the US with a frighteningly realistic view of almost 360 degrees. A second building contains the triple-level Aquarium, which takes you from above the waters of the South Florida coast to the depth of the ocean. The North and West Wings contain the rest of the permanent displays, and visiting exhibitions on six different levels, making for a lengthy visit if you hope to see everything.

Pérez Art Museum Miami

Walk right next door to the **Pérez Art Museum Miami** ❹ (1103 Biscayne Blvd; tel: 305-375-3000; http://pamm.org; Fri–Tue 10am–6pm, Thu 10am–9pm; charge). This contemporary art museum was also relocated to Museum Park, this one in 2013, when it acquired almost 500 works to expand the collection. Mexican artist Diego Rivera features alongside other Latin American artists, especially from Cuba. The museum concentrates on the 20th and 21st centuries, and also on the arts and cultures of North and South America, Africa, and Western Europe.

If you're visiting on a Saturday then there's one other attraction to see here: from the art museum walk east towards the bay and then south along the bay to the new **Miami Science Barge** (1075 Biscayne Blvd; tel: 305-912-3439; www.miamisciencebarge.org; Sat 11am–5pm; suggested donation). While it can hardly compete with the science museum, this floating marine laboratory and educational center is still a lot of fun. The aim is to encourage the development of a sustainable Miami by concentrating on the area's unique ecological system. There's an onboard farm that produces food and water and generates power, and there are talks and workshops too.

AROUND THE FREEDOM TOWER

You have two options from here: you could continue walking south along the Museum Park Baywalk, which follows the

Pérez Art Museum Miami   *An optical installation at the Pérez Art Museum Miami*

coast to become the Baywalk Path. Or you could return to the Museum Park Metromover station, hop on for three stops south and get off at Freedom Tower (see page 59). Or if you're hungry at this stage, then go one stop to Eleventh Street and diagonally opposite the station is **La Esquina at 11th Bistro Italiano**, see ❶. For something Greek then one block south, between NE 2nd Avenue and Biscayne Blvd, is **Elia Gourmet**, see ❷. From either of these you can then resume your Metromover ride to Freedom Tower.

You exit from the Freedom Tower station on NE 2nd Avenue, with the tower itself visible to the east. Walk south on the avenue to the next junction and head east on NE 6th Street, also known as Port Blvd. Ahead of you looms the unmissable shape of the **American Airlines Arena** (601 Biscayne Blvd; tel: 786-777-1000; www.aaarena.com; see page 105). Even if you don't plan to visit, it's still worth a look. This multi-million-dollar venue hosts big-scale live concerts, think Ed Sheeran, Radiohead, Lady Gaga, Barbra Streisand, U2, Celine Dion, and Madonna. It's also a sports arena and home to Miami's National Basketball Association team, Miami Heat. It can host smaller shows too, in its Waterfront Theater, which is the largest theater in Florida with a capacity for up to 5,800 people.

From the arena head for the Freedom Tower (see page 59), which houses the **MDC Museum of Art and Design** ❺ (Freedom Tower, 600 Biscayne Blvd; tel: 305-237-7700; www.mdcmoad.org). When it reopens in spring 2018, it will display the Miami–Dade College's large collection of art and design, including paintings, sculptures, prints, photographs, videos, and installations. Highlights include the Pop Art collection and the works by contemporary artists from Latin America.

The Bayside Marketplace enjoys a lovely setting

BAYSIDE

Leaving the Tower, walk south down Biscayne Blvd on the bay side of the road. As you cross Port Blvd you can't miss the huge BAYSIDE sign, but keep walking south to the pedestrian entrance of the **Bayside Marketplace** (401 Biscayne Blvd; tel: 305-577-3344; www.baysidemarket place.com; Mon–Thu 10am–10pm, Fri–Sat 10am–11pm, Sun 10am–9.30pm), a mix of shopping mall, entertainment complex, and restaurants. It leads right through to the marina, with plenty of waterfront eating options, a good choice being **Mambo Café**, see ❸. You can also take boat rides and there's a Walk of Fame with stars designed by artist Romero Britto (see page 36).

From here you can walk around the marina or return to Biscayne Blvd and walk south to **Bayfront Park** (www.bay frontparkmiami.com). This genteel park with bay views houses the Bayfront Park Amphitheater. There are regular yoga classes and even a trapeze school if you fancy ending this route on a high. If you'd rather just go for a meal, leave the park, cross Biscayne Blvd and walk west on NE 1st Street, then right on NE 3rd Avenue to sample the Peruvian delights at **Pollos and Jarras**, see ❹.

Food and Drink

❶ LA ESQUINA AT 11TH BISTRO ITALIANO

1040 Biscayne Blvd; tel: 305-381-5384; daily B, L and D; $
This casual Italian restaurant has freshly-prepared food like swordfish carpaccio, pizzas, clam pasta, and grilled fish, as well as great Italian coffee and tiramisu. At breakfast there are pastries and croissants.

❷ ELIA GOURMET

900 Biscayne Blvd #105; tel: 786-558-3542; www.eliamiami.com; daily B, L and D; $$
Top-notch Greek/Mediterranean food served in a relaxed, unfussy café-style setting with some outdoor seating. For dinner Chef Dimitri Harvalis adds some specials like *pastitsio*.

❸ MAMBO CAFÉ

Bayside Marketplace, 401 Biscayne Blvd Suite S119; tel: 305-374-7417; http://mambo cafemiami.com; daily B, L and D; $$
In among the fast-food chains at Bayside Marketplace, the lively Mambo Café stands out. It's a casual but colorful place with waterfront tables and a blend of Cuban, Caribbean, and Spanish dishes, such as paella, *mofongo*, and Cuban sandwiches.

❹ POLLOS AND JARRAS

115 NE 3rd Avenue; tel: 786-567-4940; http://pollosyjarras.com; daily L and D; $$
Don't be deterred by the bland tables outside. Inside is a colorful Peruvian bar and restaurant spread over two floors, with an extensive menu of *ceviches*, *tiraditos*, and *parrillas*… and pisco sours, of course.

The Brickell skyline

BRICKELL

The Brickell part of Downtown Miami is one of the wealthiest financial districts in the US, which has forged a flourishing scene of high-rise living, restaurants, bars, shops, and galleries to match any in the country.

DISTANCE: 4 miles (6.4km)
TIME: 1.5 hours without stops
START: Hotel Urbano
END: Brickell Key Park
POINTS TO NOTE: This is a good afternoon walk, so you can end it as the sun goes down over Biscayne Bay.

Many US downtowns can be dull, especially at night when all the workers have left. Not so in Miami's Brickell, which is as lively at night as it is busy during the day. Many of the younger workers here, pulling in hefty pay packets, live in high-rise condos and apartments close to where they work. Miami has the highest concentration of international banks in the US, and over 30,000 people live in Brickell. This has naturally resulted in restaurants and bars springing up, along with shops and art galleries.

BRICKELL AVENUE ART GALLERIES

This walk starts at the **Hotel Urbano Art Gallery** ❶ (2500 Brickell Avenue; tel: 305-854-2070; www.hotelurbanomiami. com; open access), one of the many hotels in town that doubles up as an art gallery. The hotel displays one-off, colorful works by local artists, and each season the Cuban-American artist William Braemer curates a new selection. If you stay here then all the guest rooms showcase their own exclusive artworks too.

Turn left out of the Urbano. Walking northeast along the pleasant tree-lined avenue it's hard to believe you are in the heart of a financial district. To your right are some high-rise condos, with fabulous views over the bay on the other side. Cross over to the far side to reach the exclusive **Alfa Gallery** (1627 Brickell Avenue; tel: 305-804-8685; www. alfa-gallery.com; Mon–Fri 10am–6pm, Sat 10am–8pm). This is one of the best galleries in the city, representing some of Miami's leading artists whose work can be seen in the Pérez Art Museum Miami (see page 64) and the Bass Museum of Art (see page 40) as well as in museums across the US and around the world. This light and airy gallery also enjoys bay views from the rear of the building.

A quiet lane in Simpson Park

SIMPSON PARK

Turn right out of the gallery and if you're hungry right again along SE 15th Road to **Obba Sushi**, see ❶. If not, then turn left on SE 15th Road to come to **Simpson Park** ❷ (5 SW 17th Road; tel: 305-859-2867; www.miamigov.com/parks/simpson.html; daily 8am–5pm). This is more of a small wood in the center of the city, and a lovely place to stroll in. Its full name is Simpson Park Hammock; a hammock is a term used in the southeastern US for a stand of trees, usually hardwood, that somehow stand apart from the ecological area around them. One such hammock originally ran from the Miami River south to Coconut Grove, and a section of it is preserved here in Simpson Park, named after conservationist Charles Torrey Simpson who lived in Miami for many years and had a stretch of hammock in his back garden.

Return along SE 15th Road and take the first right due north on SW 1st Avenue. A right turn on SW 13th Street takes you to **Gyu-Kaku Japanese BBQ**, see ❷. Or if you turn right along SW 12th Street you'll find **Brickell Bikes** (70 SW 12th Street; tel: 305-373-3633; www.brickellbikes.com; Mon–Fri 10am–7pm,

Sat 10am–6pm), if you want to explore on two wheels. Otherwise continue north on SW 1st and turn right on SW 10th Street for the **RedBar Brickell** (52 SW 10th Street; tel: 786-316-0303; Sun–Thu 5pm–3am, Fri–Sat 5pm–5am), a typical Brickell combination of a restaurant, bar, comedy venue, and art gallery. If it's before 5pm though you'll have to make do with **The Shops at Mary Brickell Village** ❸ (901 S Miami Avenue; tel: 305-381-6130; www.marybrickellvillage.com; Mon–Sat 10am–9pm, Sun noon–6pm) across the road. This small upscale shopping mall has boutiques, jewelers, a gym, spas, and restaurants such as the all-American **Burger and Beer Joint**, see ❸.

Brickell bangles

The River Walk Trail

Leave on the north side then right to S Miami and left to walk north to SW 8th Street. Take a right here to walk east. At Brickell Avenue cross over and left for the **Greater Miami Convention and Visitors Bureau** ❹ (701 Brickell Avenue #2700; tel: 305-539-3000; www.miamiandbeaches.com; Mon–Fri 8.30am–5pm).

RIVER WALKS

Walk north on Brickell all the way to the river where you turn right onto the **River Walk Trail**. This pleasant walk takes you past the Miami Circle, possibly a former Tequesta Indian settlement.

Beyond this is **Brickell Point**, which is close to the **Cantina La Veinte**, see ❹. The trail swings south and follows the water all the way to Brickell Key Drive where you turn left to cross the bridge to the manmade Brickell Key. Turn right when you reach Brickell Key Drive to end the walk in **Brickell Key Park** (Brickell Key Drive; tel: 305-416-1361; open access). This is only a small urban park with grassy areas and walkways, but it does offer fantastic views of Biscayne Bay, the Port of Miami, and south to Virginia Key and Key Biscayne (see page 70). If you can time your walk to end here as the sun is setting, all the better.

Food and Drink

❶ OBBA SUSHI

200 SE 15th Road; tel: 305-856-9016; http://obbasushi.com; daily L and D; $$
This smart sushi place at Brickell Harbor offers an array of soups, salads, and a wide range of sushis, sashimis, and main courses such as chicken teriyaki and lemon sea bass.

❷ GYU-KAKU JAPANESE BBQ

34 SW 13th Street Unit R1; tel: 305-400-8915; www.gyu-kaku.com/miami; daily L and D; $$
The Miami branch of this nationwide chain has a smart-casual look. An easy option if you're really hungry is the all-you-can-eat menu or at lunch a 2-course or 3-course menu, or you can pick and mix dishes like miso chili wings, Kobe-style beef or chicken garlic noodles.

❸ BURGER AND BEER JOINT

The Shops at Mary Brickell Village, 900 S Miami Avenue #130; tel: 305-523-2244; http://bnbjoint.com; daily L and D; $$
At this burger heaven you can build your own burger or choose from their range of signature or gourmet burgers, each accompanied by a craft beer recommendation. Leave room for an adult shake dessert cocktail too.

❹ CANTINA LA VEINTE

495 Brickell Avenue; tel: 786-623-6135; www.cantinala20.com; daily L and D; $$$
This colorful and smart restaurant is run by young chef Santiago Gomez, who serves up contemporary Mexican cuisine with dishes such as a Mexican shrimp and tangy *chile guajillo* soup, oysters Rockefeller, and a wide choice of dishes to share.

The best way to get around in Key Biscayne

VIRGINIA KEY AND KEY BISCAYNE BY BIKE

These offshore islands, connected by causeways, are among the favorite biking spots in Miami, so join the locals on two wheels and make the most of their beaches, parks, seaquarium, and a flurry of outdoor activities.

DISTANCE: 16 miles (26km)
TIME: A half-day
START: Alice Wainwright Park
END: Cape Florida Lighthouse
POINTS TO NOTE: Take your swimming gear with you, as you'll be passing some of the best beaches in Miami. You could also walk this route but it's at least five hours of walking, one way, though you could catch a bus back from the Cape Florida Lighthouse. A combination of driving and walking is another option, as there are some excellent hiking and biking trails on the islands. The Cape Florida Lighthouse is closed on Tuesdays and Wednesdays (limited opening hours on the other days too), although the state park remains open. Start this tour in the morning if you really want to see it.

Especially at weekends, you'll find Virginia Key and Key Biscayne busy with cyclists, hikers, kayakers, and other outdoor enthusiasts – all taking advantage of an easy way to escape the Miami high-rises, by crossing the causeways and getting out into the open space. Virginia Key is almost nothing but green spaces, and over half of Key Biscayne is the same. It would be a long old hike if you were to try to explore these places on foot from the mainland, making a bike the ideal choice to cover the ground and see these two Miami marvels.

ALICE WAINWRIGHT PARK

If you are coming across from the mainland then the perfect place to start is at the foot of the causeway to Virginia Key, at the **Alice Wainwright Park ❶** (2845 Brickell Avenue; tel: 305-416-1300; daily 6am-6pm). This is only a small park with an outdoor gym and a couple of basketball courts, but it's a nice place to hike or cycle around, with great views of the city skyline and across the water. There are palm trees and even some small cliffs. The park also has a part of the Brickell Hammock, as does Simpson Park (see page 68), the hammock being the hardwood forest that once existed between the Miami River and what is now Coconut Grove.

Off to meet Flipper the dolphin at the Miami Seaquarium

VIRGINIA KEY

Leave the park onto the Rickenbacker Causeway and take the right-hand cycle lane across the bridge to Virginia Key, enjoying the views across the water. On your right on the first spit of land you cross is the **Hobie Island Beach Park**. Nicknamed Windsurfer Beach, this is the best spot in the city for windsurfing, and there's a school here if you want to stop off and have a lesson, rent a kayak or try a paddleboard (Sailboards Miami: www.sailboardsmiami.com).

Continue on the causeway over the William M Powell Bridge to Virginia Key. On the left (take care crossing the traffic) is the **Rickenbacker Marina** (3301 Rickenbacker Causeway; tel: 305-361-1900; www.rickenbackermarina.com). There's not a lot to see there but it's pleasant to stroll around or sit and watch the coming and going of the boats, and there's a popular restaurant there too, the Rusty Pelican (see page 102). Off to the left a little further along the causeway is the **Atlantica Seafood Restaurant and Market**, see ❶.

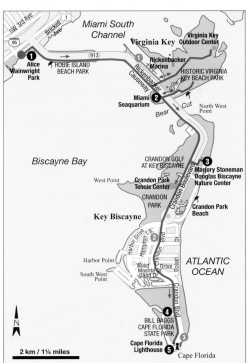

Miami Seaquarium

Keep cycling across the causeway until you reach the **Miami Seaquarium** ❷ (4400 Rickenbacker Causeway; tel: 305-361-5705; www.miamiseaquarium.com; daily 10am–6pm; charge). This large aquarium covers about 15 hectares (37 acres) and you can easily spend a few hours here. There are dolphin shows, sharks, sea lions, and crocodiles, but

for out-of-state visitors one of the more interesting displays is of the fascinating manatees that live off Florida's coast. There's also a tropical fish aquarium, killer whale shows, tropical birds, and penguins. Plan ahead and you can swim with the seals or be a trainer for a day. There are plenty of eating places too.

Outdoor fun

On the far side of the causeway from the seaquarium is the sprawling, wooded **Historic Virginia Key Beach Park** (4020 Virginia Beach Drive; tel: 305-960-4600; http://virginiakeybeachpark.net; daily 7am–sunset), with some excellent biking and hiking trails, including coastal trails and nature trails. There's also a mountain biking area towards the northern tip of the island. Kids can enjoy a playground, a carousel, and a mini-train ride, and everyone can enjoy the long beach. Birdwatchers should look out for herons, egrets, pelicans, lots of waders and seagulls, and with luck the beautiful roseate spoonbill.

Also towards the northern end of Virginia Key, close to the inlet known as Lamar Lake, is the **Virginia Key Outdoor Center** (3801 Rickenbacker Causeway; tel: 786-224-4777; www.vkoc.net; Mon–Fri 9am–6pm, Sat–Sun 8am–6pm). If you've driven to Virginia Key then you should head here to rent bikes for the day, and get out onto the island's trails. The center also hires out kayaks and provides kayak and paddleboard lessons. Kids can learn how to ride bikes, adults can enjoy kayak and paddleboard fishing and spe-

cial events include kayaking or paddle-boarding under the full moon. It's also a good place to pick up literature about the island's hiking trails and bike trails, and about activities around Miami generally.

KEY BISCAYNE

Return to the causeway and continue on to Key Biscayne, looking out on the left for the **Fossilized Reef View**. This small reef stretches along the shore for about 400 yards/metres and out to sea for over 100 yards (91 metres) and is composed of the fossilised roots of mangrove trees. It doesn't look very exciting but it is a unique feature and has provided an excellent home for crabs and other marine life.

Marjory Stoneman Douglas
Biscayne Nature Center

From the reef you can head south on paths through the woods, or return to the main road, now called Crandon Blvd and head south. Either way you will come to the **Marjory Stoneman Douglas Biscayne Nature Center ❸** (6747 Crandon Blvd; tel: 305-361-6767; www.biscayne naturecenter.org; daily 10am–4pm; donation). This lovely place is beautifully set among trees and overlooking the sand dunes and the ocean. One of the aims of the center is getting children to understand, care for and get involved with the local environment. There are organized hikes, lectures, displays on the area's natural history, hands-on exhibits, talks, and an art gallery. The center also has a pro-

The lovely white sands of Crandon Park Beach

gram to reintroduce baby sea turtles back into the wild. Marjory Stoneman Douglas was a campaigning journalist and ardent environmentalist who worked tirelessly to protect the Everglades, in particular, and the nature center is a fine testimony to her life and work.

To the lighthouse

South of the center a lovely long stretch of beach begins, while the road takes you south through Crandon Park, then through the little town of Key Biscayne. A few blocks in, look on your right for the **Ayesha Saffron Indian Restaurant**, see ②. The road goes out the other side of Key Biscayne into the **Bill Baggs Cape Florida State Park** ④ (1200 Crandon Blvd; tel: 305-361-5811; www.floridastateparks.org/park/Cape-Florida; daily 8am–sundown; charge). The beach extends all the way down here along the eastern coast of the island, and you can either head there or explore the trails plying this wooded park.

At the southern end is the **Cape Florida Lighthouse** ⑤ (1200 S Crandon Blvd; tel: 305-361-5811; www.floridastateparks.org/park/Cape-Florida; free guided tours Thu–Mon 10–11am and 1–2pm). Built in 1825, then rebuilt in 1846, this is the oldest standing structure in Miami–Dade County. Unfortunately it cannot be visited except on one of the guided tours, but it's a beautiful place to end your tour. For a well-deserved refreshment, head north to the **Lighthouse Café**, see ③.

Food and Drink

① ATLANTICA SEAFOOD RESTAURANT & MARKET

3501 Rickenbacker Causeway; tel: 305-361-0177; www.atlanticafishrestaurant.com; Tue–Sun L and D; $$$
Honduran chef Marvin Garcia oversees the menu at this smart-casual place overlooking the water. There's a choice of sandwiches, tacos, seafood baskets, or the catch of the day.

② AYESHA SAFFRON INDIAN RESTAURANT

328 Crandon Blvd, Key Biscayne; tel: 786-953-4761; http://ayeshakeybiscayne.com; Tue–Sun L and D; $$

This white-tablecloth place with colorful walls is a chance to try delicately-flavored Indian dishes such as samosas, biryanis and tandoori dishes, alongside such favorites as chicken tikka masala, lamb vindaloo, and fish curry.

③ LIGHTHOUSE CAFÉ

Bill Baggs Cape Florida State Park, 1200 Crandon Blvd, Key Biscayne; tel: 305-361-8487; www.lighthouserestaurants.com; daily B, L and early D; $$
Set back from the beach but with an oceanfront view this casual place serves everything from breakfast toast through to soups, salads, and sandwiches, or full meals such as fried shrimp, grilled Florida lobster, the Cuban *ropa vieja*, and a full drinks menu.

COCONUT GROVE

*Sparkling as much in the sun as under the stars, and once a writers'
and artists' colony, bohemian Coconut Grove has fantastic festivals,
savvy stores, and a breezy night–time buzz.*

DISTANCE: 5.2 miles (8.4km)
TIME: A half-day
START: Vizcaya Museum and Gardens
END: Merrie Christmas Park
POINTS TO NOTE: On Saturday
nights you can join in the Coconut
Grove Art Walk, when galleries
stay open late and some provide
entertainment, wine, and nibbles.
On the first Saturday of the month
there's a fashion, art and music night
at the CocoWalk shopping mall. On
the last weekend of the year Coconut
Grove hosts the King Mango Strut
Parade (www.kingmangostrut.org),
a wacky event that started in 1982
as a counterpart to the King Orange
Parade, which ended in 2002 but
King Mango struts on! The Vizcaya
Museum and Gardens are closed on
Tuesdays, as is the Barnacle Historic
State Park. You can take the Metrorail
to the start of this route, Vizcaya. You
could also do this tour by bike to cut
down on the 30-minute walk between
the first two attractions.

Coconut Grove is southwest of Brickell
and the Downtown area, and only two
stops from the Brickell station on the
Metrorail service. It's the oldest continuously-inhabited part of the city, and as
such is where Miami City Hall is located.
Miami has long been known for welcoming immigrants but in fact the first arrivals settled in Coconut Grove in 1825.
Later arrivals came from Europe, the
Bahamas, and the northeast US. Coconut Grove was incorporated as an independent city in 1919, but this didn't last
long as it became part of Miami in 1925.

This feeling of being part of Miami, but
not really, has persisted over the years,
and Coconut Grove remains an alternative kind of a place. In the 1960s it was to
Miami what Haight-Ashbury was to San
Francisco, the center of the hippy move-
ment and a focus for alternative culture.
It's where artists, writers, and musicians
head for when they go to Miami. Even
if Coconut Grove didn't have this history and a laid-back feel, it would still
be one of the most beautiful places to
walk in Miami. Although this is a half-day
tour, you may want to stretch it to a day

The grand, Renaissance-style Vizcaya Museum and Gardens

to explore everything and to enjoy that relaxed feel to the full.

VIZCAYA MUSEUM AND GARDENS

The tour starts close to the start of two other tours, Brickell (see page 67) and the bike tour to Virginia Key and Key Biscayne (see page 70). It also begins close to the Vizcaya stop on Miami's Metrorail system. Take the Vizcaya Museum exit, then it's a 10-minute walk to the **Vizcaya Museum and Gardens** ❶ (3251 S Miami Avenue; tel: 305-250-9133; www.vizcaya.org; Wed–Mon 9.30am–4.30pm; charge). Formerly known as the Villa Vizcaya, it was once the winter home of James Deering, a businessman, socialite, and avid collector of antiques. His original estate was much larger, as it also included the Mercy Hospital, now on separate land to the south of the villa. The villa itself was built between 1914 and 1922, and was named after the province of Vizcaya in northern Spain, which in English is Biscay, and hence the Bay of Biscay. Because Miami is on Biscayne Bay, Deering thought it an appropriate name. On his death in 1926 his estate went to two of his nieces, but eventually due to difficulties of economics and upkeep, the villa and its grounds passed to Miami–Dade County.

The grounds cover about 20 hectares (50 acres) and include some of the native hardwood forest that remains in the city of Miami, as Deering was also a conservationist. The landscaped grounds are inspired by the designs of formal European gardens from the 17th and 18th centuries and are decorated with sculptures from Deering's collection. Inside the house the collection is even more remarkable, ranging from Chinese ceramics to Renaissance tapestries. Miami boasts some impressive residencies, but none to rival this one.

GREEN MIAMI

Leaving the museum, turn left to walk southwest down S Miami Avenue. It's a 30-minute walk to the next attraction on this route, but a pleasant walk with trees lining both sides of the street for much of the way. Alternatively you can return to the Vizcaya Metrorail stop and take the train to the next station, Coconut Grove, though it's still a 15-minute walk. If approaching from the museum, S Miami Avenue becomes S Bayshore Drive, and shortly after on your left is **David T. Kennedy Park** (2400 S Bayshore Drive; tel: 305-416-1133; open access), which stands between S Bayshore Drive and Biscayne Bay. Kennedy was a former mayor of Miami and this lovely 12-hectare (29 acres) park has walking trails, plenty of shade, picnic spots, an outdoor gym, a children's playground, a dog park, and beach volleyball courts. There are free yoga classes at the weekends, Citi Bike docking stations (see page 117) and the bay views are totally free.

David T. Kennedy Park

Keep walking southwest along Bayshore Drive and on your left just before the junction with Aviation Avenue in a row of buildings is **Monty's Raw Bar**, see ❶, a perfect pit-stop for a refreshing drink. Otherwise keep going and by turning left on Charthouse Drive you reach **Grove Key Marina** (3385 Pan American Drive; tel: 305-858-6527; http://groveharbourmarina.com). Like many marinas the main attraction is wandering around and looking at the waterside activity, but you can also find restrooms here and a Fresh market store if you want to buy drinks or snacks.

Another few minutes southwest along S Bayshore Drive brings you to the **Kenneth M. Myers Bayside Park** (open access). This is another of Coconut Grove's pleasant little parks, with shady palm trees, some fun outdoor sculptures, and bay views. On its own it may not amount to too much, but together with all of the neighborhood's other parks and open spaces, it's the reason why Coconut Grove is the greenest part of Miami.

Peacock Park

At the end of this park where S Bayshore Drive swings to the right, walk

Monty's Raw Bar   *Coconut Grove shopping*

straight ahead and into **Peacock Park** ❷ (2820 McFarlane Road; tel: 305-443-2604; open access). This is a perfect place if you have children as there are two separate play areas, one for toddlers and one for older children. It has a skating park, a tennis court, a baseball field and a basketball field, and with its location by the sea and its proximity to the center of Coconut Grove it is incredibly well-used by locals. It's also of great historic significance. The park is named after Charles and Isabella Peacock, who built a hotel on this spot in 1886, one of the first hotels in Florida. People who came on vacation ended up staying, and immigrants from the Bahamas came to work at the hotel, creating one of the area's first black communities. It was essentially the start of Coconut Grove, and it's been a public park since the land was bought by the city of Miami in 1934.

Adjacent to the northwest end of Peacock Park is **St Stephen's Episcopal Church** (2750 McFarlane Road; tel: 305-448-2601; http://sseccg.org). The church can trace its roots back to 1886 when an English couple settled here as Coconut Grove was in its infancy. They raised money for a church that was built in 1912, in another location. The present church was consecrated in 1959, and was a result of the many armed forces that were stationed here during World War II. The old church couldn't cope with the increase in the congregations and planning for a new one began.

COCOWALK

Exit the church onto McFarlane Road and straight ahead at the junction with Grand Avenue is **CocoWalk** ❸ (3015 Grand Avenue; tel: 305-444-0777; www.cocowalk.net; daily 10am–11pm). This small shopping mall is a focal point for local activity, even though it only has about 30 stores, including Gap and Victoria's Secret. It also has numerous restaurants and bars, and a movie theater, and on the first Saturday of each month it plays host to a night of fashion, art, and music. A good lunch or dinner option is **Jaguar**, see ❷, or sports fans may prefer the **Sandbar Sports Grill**, see ❸, on the other side of Grand Avenue.

MORE PARKS

From the road junction outside the Coco-Walk entrance head southwest down Main Highway. Another shopping and entertainment center is off to your right along **Commodore Plaza**, with galleries and other stores but mainly eating places, including sidewalk seating if you want to dine al fresco. A little further along Main Highway, on the right, is **The Barnacle Historic State Park** ❹ (3485 Main Highway; tel: 305-442-6866; www.floridastateparks.org/park/The-Barnacle; Wed–Mon 9am–5pm; charge). The Barnacle is the house within the park, built in 1891 and the oldest building in Miami–Dade County that's still

The Barnacle, Ralph Middleton Munroe's former house

in its original location. It was the home of Ralph Middleton Munroe, a yacht designer, naturalist, and photographer, and gives a fascinating glimpse into what life was like at that time, when all traffic into Coconut Grove came on the water.

Keep walking southwest down Main Highway for about twenty minutes, and at the end turn left for **The Kampong** ❺ (4013 Douglas Road; tel: 305-442-7169; www.ntbg.org/gardens/kampong. php; Mon–Fri 9am–5pm, Sat 10am–2pm; charge). This tropical botanical garden covering 3.6 hectares (9 acres) is one of five gardens run by the National Tropical Botanical Garden, based in Hawaii. It's a rich and diverse garden, filled with tropical plants and trees from all over the world, amassed over the last hundred years or so. There are fruit trees, palm trees, flowering trees, bamboo, and of course countless brightly-colored flowering plants. Allow plenty of time to explore – keen photographers will need even more time.

On leaving the Kampong turn left onto Douglas Road, veer right onto Ingraham Highway, and right again onto Hardie Avenue. When you reach SW 42nd Avenue/S Le Jeune Road turn left and this brings you to **Merrie Christmas Park** (4355 SW 42nd Avenue; tel: 305-416-1300; open access). Randall Norton "Randy" Christmas was the Mayor of Miami from 1955–57, and later, when his daughter Merrie sadly passed away at the age of only 15, he acquired this land to be kept as a park for the people

in her memory. The sound of children playing in the park is a poignant tribute to Merrie Christmas.

Food and Drink

❶ MONTY'S RAW BAR

2550 S Bayshore Drive; tel: 305-856-3992; www.montysrawbar.com; daily L and D; $$$

This lively seafood place is a legendary local hangout if you want to relax and have oysters from the raw bar, great chowders, fresh-caught fish, fish and chips, stone crab claws or even steaks and pizza. The food is good without being gourmet, as it's all about the atmosphere.

❷ JAGUAR

3067 Grand Avenue; tel: 305-444-0216; www.jaguarspot.jaguarhg.com; daily L and D; $$–$$$

In among the fast-food places of CocoWalk is this fun and casual Latino restaurant. Some of the chef's specials include roasted pork belly with lentils, and shrimp mango-verde.

❸ SANDBAR SPORTS GRILL

3064 Grand Avenue; tel: 305-444-5270; http://sandbargrove.com; daily L and D; $$

Don't come here if you want a quiet romantic dinner, but do come if you want a sports bar atmosphere with decent, affordable food such as tequila fajitas, tacos, burgers, burritos, beers, and cocktails.

A family ride on the Shark Valley Tour Trail

THE EVERGLADES BY BIKE

Just two hours' drive from Miami is the untamed heart of Florida – a swamp rich in wildlife and as raw in nature as the entire peninsula used to be. And traveling by bike is an exhilarating way to soak in this wonderful ecosystem.

DISTANCE: 15 miles (24.1km), plus 4.6 mile (7.4km) diversion to visit Miccosukee Indian Village and Miccosukee Indian School
TIME: A half-day
START: Shark Valley Tram Tours
END: Shark Valley Tram Tours
POINTS TO NOTE: For group tours contact Shark Valley Tram Tours. You can also rent a bike with them too – book ahead as the place does get busy. Shark Valley is about 40 miles (64km) west of Downtown Miami, and not accessible by public transportation so you will need to come by car or taxi. If you drive, remember that the car park closes at 6pm so allow plenty of time to get back. There are no short cuts on the loop road so you either go the whole way or turn round and head back. By Florida law if you're under 16 you must wear a bike helmet. Check the weather forecast before heading out. As a rule, it's usually best to bike in the morning, when it's cooler and you're more likely to see wildlife. You pay a fee to enter the National Park, but the ticket is valid for seven days.

The Everglades actually begin near Orlando, over 200 miles (322km) north of Miami, giving you some idea of their scale. They start with Lake Okeechobee, the largest lake contained within any of the Lower 48 states. This is a vast expanse of 730 square miles (1891 sq km), and yet its average depth is only about 9ft (2.7m). As a result of this, during the rainy season when water washes out of the lake and flows south, it forms a shallow body of water some 60 miles (97km) wide which makes its way slowly to join the waters that surround southern Florida. The result, every year, is the creation of a wetland that covers almost 2,400 square miles (6,216 sq km), about the size of the state of Delaware.

The Everglades contain a wealth of wildlife (see box page 80), and even on this half-day bike excursion you're sure to see some of them, including what everyone wants to see in Florida: 'gators. Spotting them while cycling or walking is far more exciting than if in the company of lots of other people on a tour bus or tram (see box page 82).

A 'gator encounter

SHARK VALLEY VISITOR CENTER

The easiest way to visit the Everglades is to head due west out of Miami, and drive to the **Shark Valley Visitor Center** ❶ (36000 SW 8th Street; tel: 305-221-8776; www.nps.gov/ever/planyourvisit/svdirections.htm; daily mid–Dec to mid–Apr 8.30am–5pm, rest of year 9am–5pm; charge). Here you can watch a video and see displays about the Everglades, pick up literature, buy postcards and souvenirs, find out if there are any special events like talks or guided hikes, and check a map of the route you're about to do… though it's a single loop road and impossible to get lost on if you stay on it, as you should.

Adjacent to the visitor center is **Shark Valley Tram Tours** (36000 SW 8th Street; tel: 305-221-8455; www.sharkvalleytramtours.com; daily 8am–5pm). This company rents bikes for self-guided tours, and also offers tram tours if you prefer to join a group and have an informative tour leader. Tram tours are hourly every day from December to April, then four times a day the rest of the year. Booking is recommended. You can also buy snacks and drinks here if you didn't bring enough with you. Make sure you're well-stocked with water, to cope with the Florida heat and humidity. You'll also be exercising, causing you to lose even more body liquid through perspiration.

THE TRAIL

All you need to do then is to set off on the trail, one end of which is east of

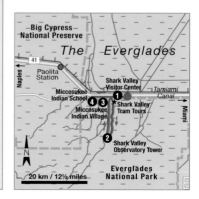

Everglades wildlife

Living here are more than 400 species of birds, 125 species of fish, 60 species of reptiles and amphibians, 25 species of mammals, over 120 species of trees, 1,000 species of seed-bearing plants, and 24 species of orchids, including the rare ghost orchid. The Everglades is the only place in the US where you'll find both crocodiles and alligators living side by side. Crocodiles (distinguished from alligators by a spade-shaped snout and two visible sets of teeth rather than one) are one of 14 endangered species protected here. Others are Florida panthers, West Indian manatees, Cable Sable sea sparrows, and wood storks.

Heron on the trail   *The Shark Valley Observation Tower*

the visitor center, the other end west of Shark Valley Tram Tours. It doesn't matter which way you go as it's a looped trail and you'll still see everything and end up back where you started. There's also a short looped nature trail you can hike from here, the Otter Cave Hammock Trail, and you may wish to do this before you pick up your bikes or after you drop them off as they're not allowed on the trail. It's about a half-mile (0.8km) to where the trail starts, along the trail you're going to take anyway, and although it's only a quarter-mile (0.4km) long it takes you through some of the remaining hardwood forest, known as a hammock (see page 68), over bridges that cross a stream, then back to the visitor center, hopefully seeing some wildlife along the way. Be warned that this trail can sometimes be flooded during the summer, so ask about trail conditions at the visitor center.

Set off cycling due south in either direction and take care because you'll be sharing the trail with other cyclists, hikers and the occasional tram that comes lumbering by, although these are only once an hour even in peak season. Sometimes your fellow travelers will irritate you by talking loudly, not realising that this alerts and scares off the wildlife. At other times you'll be delighted when other people share their sightings with you, tell you where you might see something, or alert you to the fact that something is there because they're standing watching intently or looking through binoculars at something.

The something may well be an alligator, or a group of 'gators, and while this can be startling for anyone who's never seen them before, they are a part of the landscape here. They are nothing to be alarmed about, but they are still something to be treated with respect and a little caution (see box). If you see one moving then it's best to stop and watch where it's going, and let it get there. There's no arguing with a 'gator. If you see one lying at the side of the trail, stop and think if you can get by without getting too close to the creature. If one is lying right across the path then there may be nothing for it but to turn around and try riding the other way round the trail. Do not go off the trail to get around, as there may be others you can't see. It's not unknown for people to come across groups of 'gators which have decided to sun themselves right on the trail, completely clocking the way. You either wait for them to move, which could take hours, or you turn around.

Shark Valley Observatory Tower

If you're not halted by 'gators (and most people aren't), then you'll know when you're roughly half-way round the trail when you get to the **Shark Valley Observatory Tower ❷**. You can see this from a long way away as it's a concrete structure that looms 40-feet (12m) over

Warning sign

the flat landscape around. Designed by Florida architect Edward M. Ghezzi, opinion is divided on whether it's a beautifully flowing creation or a rather ugly intrusion on the natural landscape. What's undeniable is that it does give you a breathtaking 360-degree view across the Everglades, with the chance to gaze down at the pools surrounding the tower and watch the alligators that are almost certain to be there. The tower has another attraction, as it's the only place on the way round where there are restrooms.

It's now time to change direction and start cycling north back towards the visitor center. When wildlife is concerned there's no saying what you might see, as it depends on the time of year and the weather, and several other factors. Not the least of these is patience on your part. If you find a quiet spot where you want to pause for a rest, just stand quietly and wait and let the wildlife come to you. With birds you may well see different species of heron, egrets, perhaps storks, and roseate spoonbills. Ducks, geese, and waders are common. There are numerous hawks around, and you might see golden eagles and turkey vultures too. Many of these birds are looking for frogs, toads and newts, and so should you, though not with the same purpose in mind. There are turtles, terrapins and tortoises, but also plenty of snakes around, some of them poisonous... so treat these with care, just as you would the 'gators.

Alligators

If you see an alligator while you're cycling or hiking, don't panic. It's very rare of them to attack humans, provided you keep your distance. Stay at least 15 feet (5m) away, and don't move towards them. The incidents that do occur are usually because the animal was startled when people accidentally get close without seeing the creature, or when people deliberately approach too close, causing it to feel threatened and defend itself and its territory. It goes without saying that you do not feed them. The way to create a dangerous alligator is to start feeding it. Also, some people think it would be a great idea to stand near an alligator to have their picture taken. This is not a great idea.

MICCOSUKEE INDIAN VILLAGE AND SCHOOL

If you have time before returning to the visitor center and taking your bike back, you should definitely consider cycling north to the main road and turning left to the **Miccosukee Indian Village ❸** and further on to the **Miccosukee Indian School ❹**. About 300–400 Miccosukee Indians still live on their reservation here, which is much larger than the impression you might get from visiting here. This is

Don't get too close　　　　　　　　　　　　*Miccosukee Indian Village*

naturally the tourist face of the tribe, who have arts and crafts for sale. The Miccosukee originally lived in what is now Georgia but were pushed into northern and then southern Florida because of the advancement of European settlers. They were also originally a part of the Seminole nation but they were eventually recognised as a distinct tribe in the mid-20th century. Their story can be read about in the Cultural Center here, bringing another dimension to the tour when you consider how the Miccosukee made their lives here among the wildlife and wetness of the Everglades.

Food and Drink

There are no eating places in Shark Valley, though you can buy snacks and soft drinks at Shark Valley Tram Tours. If you want to take the opportunity to sample alligator, though, you'll find it on restaurant menus around Miami. Here are some suggestions:

COOPERTOWN AIRBOAT RIDES AND RESTAURANT

22700 SW 8th Street; tel: 305-226-6048; http://coopertownairboats.com; daily 9am–5pm; $$

On the way to or from the start of this tour you'll pass Coopertown, whose bustling country-style restaurant always has gator tail on the menu, along with catfish and other southern and Florida specialties.

KUSH

2003 N Miami Avenue; tel: 305-576-4500; http://kushwynwood.com; Sun–Thu noon–11pm, Fri–Sat 11.30am–1am; $$

If you like craft beer, gastropubs with art on the wall and you want to try alligator, this Wynwood bar ticks all the boxes. One of their regular starters is Florida alligator bites served with creamy garlic and spicy mayo.

LOKAL

3190 Commodore Plaza; tel: 305-442-3377; www.lokalmiami.com; Mon–Tue noon–10pm, Wed–Fri noon–11pm, Sat 11.30am–11pm, Sun 11.30am–10pm; $$

On Commodore Plaza in Coconut Grove (see page 77), LoKal's casual burgers and beer look belies food that uses quality local ingredients - including fresh alligator strips - and an impressive selection of local craft beers on tap.

PIT BAR-B-Q

16400 SW 8th Street; tel: 305-226-2272; www.thepitbarbq.com; Mon–Thu 11am–9pm, Fri–Sun 11am–midnight; $$

Driving to Shark Valley you'll pass right by this buzzing place with its wood-burning pit BBQ and its regular starter of gator legs, though you can also have the less common and more hearty 'gator rib dinner.

Christ of the Abyss

TO THE FLORIDA KEYS

If you think the keys in Miami's Biscayne Bay are attractive,
take a car and head south through the main keys from Key Largo
to Key West for one of the most exhilarating drives in the US.

DISTANCE: 200 miles (322km)
TIME: 4–5 hours one-way, without stops
START: Miami
END: Key West
POINTS TO NOTE: For the full Keys experience, then instead of returning on Highway 1, keep driving through Key Largo to North Key Largo. Here you can see both the Crocodile Lake National Wildlife Refuge and the Key Largo Hammock State Botanical Site before taking County Road 905A back to the mainland and re-joining Highway 1 to Miami. You could drive to Key West and back to Miami in a day but it would be a long day. It's better to stay overnight.

Many of the islands off Miami are man-made, and the natural ones like Key Biscayne are not a part of the string of islands known as the Florida Keys. These are a distinct group of islands sitting on tops of coral reefs and are more properly called cays. They arc around in a gentle crescent to form the most south-ernly part of the United States, with the Atlantic Ocean on one side and the Gulf of Mexico on the other. The classic drive starts when you cross over to Key Largo in the north, about an hour's drive from Miami, and head south on Highway 1, which turns into the Overseas Highway, all the way to Key West.

KEY LARGO

The first of the Florida Keys, reached from the mainland on Highway 1, is **Key Largo ❶**. This is the name of both the island and the town, and it's here that Highway 1 becomes the Overseas Highway, which acts as one long main street. Key Largo is still known for the 1948 movie of the same name, in which Humphrey Bogart and Lauren Bacall confront a killer hurricane. All that remains of those nostalgic Bogie days is the **Caribbean Club Bar** (MM 104), where a few scenes are said to have been filmed, and the original **African Queen**, from Bogart's 1951 film, is down the road.

One of the highlights here is on your left as you drive south: the **John Pen-**

Idyllic Key Largo   *Resident pelicans in Islamorada*

nekamp Coral Reef State Park (Mile Marker 102.5; tel: 305-451-1202; www.pennekamppark.com; daily 8am–sunset; charge), the country's first undersea park, established in 1963. Here, a 78 sq mile (200 sq km) coral reef extends 3 miles (5km) into the ocean, providing a home for nearly 600 species of fish. The park offers glass-bottom boat rides, sailing and snorkeling tours aboard a 38ft (12 meter) catamaran, and kayak rentals. It also conducts a range of scuba lessons and dives, including to the Key Largo Dry Rocks, where the *Christ of the Deep*, a replica of Guido Galletti's statue *Christ of the Abyss* (in the Mediterranean Sea off Genoa, Italy) lies submerged surrounded by a coral reef.

For a bite to eat, stop off at the characterful **Mrs Mac's Kitchen,** see ❶.

WINDLEY KEY

Continue driving on south, passing over **Plantation Key** before reaching **Windley Key**. On your left look out for the **Island Grill,** see ❷, a great place to lunch. Further on, at the **Windley Key Fossil Reef Geological State Park** (MM 85; tel: 305-664-2540; visitor center: Thu–Mon 8am–5pm; charge) there's a rare opportunity to see 125,000-year-old fossilized specimens of coral animals.

ISLAMORADA

Continuing south is **Islamorada** ❷ – actually one community that straddles several keys hence its nickname the Village of Islands.

The **Theater of the Sea** (MM 84.5; tel: 305-664-2431; www.theaterofthesea.com; reservation desk: daily 10am–5pm; charge) has been in business on Islamorada since 1946 hosting sea lion and dolphin shows, glass-bottom boat rides, and a shark pit. Reserve well in advance if you want to do the Dolphin Adventure package, which includes a swim with the dolphins, and the similar sea lion and stingray swims. Younger children and those less comfortable in deep water can wade with the animals for a lower price.

At the southern end of town, the **Hurricane Monument** (MM 81.6) commemorates the people who died in the Labor Day hurricane of 1935 – still the most intense hurricane ever to hit the US.

Seven Mile Bridge
Beyond here the keys are smaller and more spread out for a while, as you pass over **Duck Key**, **Vaca Key** and **Boot Key** before driving across the **Seven Mile Bridge**. Although actually just a shade under 7 miles (11km) it is the longest between-island stretch you can drive in the Keys. Completed in 1982, it runs over a channel between the Gulf of Mexico and the Straits of Florida. Paralleling it is the original bridge built for Flagler's railroad. The trains ran until the hurricane of 1935 ruined the roadbed and the Great Depression ruined the economy, making an automobile route the more practical alternative.

PIGEON KEY

The old railroad bridge leads to **Pigeon Key**, off to your right as you cross the Overseas Highway. If you want to visit you'll need to backtrack to the town of Marathon and take a guided tour by ferry. Henry Flagler built housing on Pigeon Key to shelter the workers he brought to Florida to work on his Overseas Railroad. Several of the structures survive and are part of a tour that leaves from the **Pigeon Key Visitors Center** (MM 48; tel: 305-743-5999; www.pigeonkey.net; departures at 10am, noon and 2pm; charge). A film tells the fascinating story of Mr. Flagler and Flagler's Folly and the railroad he built from Miami to Key West in spite of huge obstacles.

BAHIA HONDA KEY

The Seven Mile Bridge reaches the **Bahia Honda Key** and the **Bahia Honda State Park** (MM 37; tel: 305-872-2353; www.bahiahondapark.com; daily 8am–sunset; charge). Here are two of the best beaches on the Keys: Calusa Beach, next to the Bahia Honda Bridge, and the mile-long (1.6kms) Sandspur Beach. You can rent a sun longer for the afternoon, camp out for a night, go fishing, diving, or kayaking. The highlight of a visit is a snorkeling tour out to **Looe Key National Marine Sanctuary**, whose 5 mile (8km) stretch of reef is one of the world's most sensational aquatic showcases. You can also buy snacks and drinks and there are rental cabins if you want to stay longer.

BIG PINE KEY AND BEYOND

Beyond is **Big Pine Key** ❸, home to the **Springer's Bar and Grill**, see ❸, and the **National Key Deer Refuge** (visitor center at MM 30.5; Big Pine Shopping Center, 28950 Watson Blvd; tel: 305-872-0774;

The Seven Mile Bridge and the lovely stretch of beach along the Bahia-Honda State Park

www.fws.gov/refuge/National_Key_Deer_Refuge: daily sunrise–sunset). The diminutive Key deer live on about 20 of the islands. In earlier days, hunters, developers, and automobiles reduced the population to less than 50, but efforts at the refuge – including strictly enforced speed limits – have boosted their numbers into the hundreds. Some of the deer are quite used to humans and may come close, but do not feed them. Turn right near MM 30 onto Key Deer Boulevard to the Blue Hole, a flooded quarry that attracts both deer and alligators.

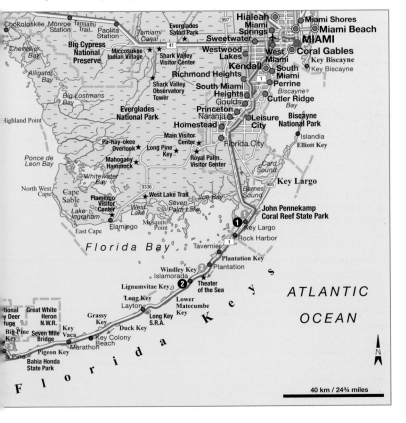

Cycling in Key West

Off Big Pine Key is **No Name Key**, but to show they didn't run out of names there are many more keys to cross as you continue on, now heading west. The **Torch Keys** are named after their flammable trees. A short distance offshore is a private island home to the exclusive Little Palm Island Resort and Spa. The restaurant, however, is open to the public and accessible by a ferry from Little Torch Key. **Summerland Key** offers scenic side roads if you want to get off the Highway for a while, and **Cudjoe Key** has modern campsites for large trailers. On **Sugar Loaf Key**, turn right just past MM 17 to view Perky's bat tower, built in 1929 to house bats in the hope they would swallow the island's mosquito problem, but once released, they never returned.

The **Saddlebunch Keys** are little more than a series of mangrove outcroppings. **Big Coppit**, **Rockland**, and **East Rockland** house the servicemen of the US Naval Air Station on **Boca Chica Key**. **Stock Island** serves as a suburb of Key West and is the home of the Tennessee Williams Performing Arts Center (tel: 305-295-7676; www.twstages.com).

KEY WEST

Crossing the next bridge, you have literally reached the end of the road, **Key West ❹**. The character of Key West derives from its history as a haven for transients. Its proximity to the American mainland and the West Indies has introduced many different influences that have merged into something totally unique. The Calusa Indians managed to get to this speck 100 miles (160km) from the Florida peninsula. The Spanish were the first Europeans to build settlements here, but Indians and pirates made life dangerous. The settlement became part of the US in 1821 when Florida was ceded by Spain. In 1845 the government began constructing a Naval Base (now called Truman Annex) and in 1866 completed **Fort Zachary Taylor A** (Southard St; tel: 305-292-6713; www.floridastateparks.org; daily 8am–sunset, fort closes 5pm; charge), now a museum of Civil War artifacts. The **East Martello Museum and Gallery** (3501 S. Roosevelt Blvd; tel: 305-296-3913; www.kwahs.

The Dry Tortugas

To reach the westernmost of the islands, you have to travel by boat or seaplane to the **Dry Tortugas**, 68 miles (109km) away. The name told 16th-century mariners that the island was "dry", as in there was no fresh water; *tortugas*, Spanish for turtles, meant there was no fresh meat. There wasn't much on the island until 1846 when the US government started work on the Tortugas' Garden Key to create Fort Jefferson – the "Gibraltar of the Gulf" – and provide a haven for American vessels. Abandoned in 1874, the fort is now the **Dry Tortugas National Park** (for ferry information, tel: 305-292-6100; www.fortjefferson.com; departures daily at 8am, return at 5pm; charge).

The iconic Sloppy Joe's

Fort Jefferson, Dry Tortugas National Park

com; daily 9.30am–4.305pm; charge) was one of two towers that were begun – but never completed – to help defend the fort. Today it houses local-history exhibits.

Old Town has some 3,000 historic buildings, as well as Mallory Square and the Historic Seaport. There are two ways to get an overview of the island: the venerable Conch Train (tel: 305-294-5161; www.conchtourtrain.com) and the Old Town Trolley (tel: 305-296-6688; www.historictours.com). The trolley allows riders to hop-on and off along the route. Both leave every 30 minutes from different locations. If Old Town is the heart of Key West, Mallory Square is its commercial soul. Throngs of visitors gather here every evening for the famous Sunset Celebration.

Hemingway's legacy

Key West's claim to fame is the Hemingway connection. At the corner of Greene and Duval streets is the famous **Sloppy Joe's**. Touted as one of Ernest Hemingway's favorite bars when he lived here from 1931 to 1940, Joe's also plays host to the popular Hemingway Days in July. Purists will want to visit **Captain Tony's Saloon** (428 Greene St), the oldest licensed saloon in Florida. Hemingway would stroll down here from his home, now the **Hemingway Home and Museum** (907 Whitehead St; tel: 305-294-1136; www.hemingwayhome.com; daily 9am–5pm; charge). This is where he wrote *To Have and Have Not*. Descendants of his six-toed cats still have the run of the place. Nearby, the **Six Toed Cat** is a good place for a fish lunch, see ④.

Food and Drink

❶ MRS MAC'S KITCHEN

99336 Overseas Highway, Key Largo; tel: 305-451-3722; www.mrsmacskitchen.com; Mon–Sat B, L and D; $$

Serving food since 1947, it's plain old-fashioned home cooking, think conch chowder and chili. The key lime pie is a treat.

❷ ISLAND GRILL

85501 Overseas Highway, Islamorada; tel: 305-664-8400; http://keysislandgrill.com; daily B, L and D; $$

This unassuming place is known for its tuna nachos but the seafood choice is wide: clams, scallops, fresh shrimps, and the catch of the day. Save some space for the key lime pie. Live music in the evenings.

❸ SPRINGER'S BAR AND GRILL

31251 Avenue A, Big Pine Key; tel: 305-872-3022; http://springersbar.com; Tue–Sun L and D; $$

Enjoy coconut shrimp, conch chowder, burgers, and pizza, as well as three choices of pot pie on an outdoor patio. Live music.

❹ SIX TOED CAT

823 Whitehead Street, Key West; tel: 305-294-3318; www.sixtoedcatkeywest.com; daily B and L; $$

The fish here comes straight from the boat and you can have a fish sandwich or the catch of the day, but there's also paninis, salads, cakes, and an all-day breakfast.

DIRECTORY

Hand-picked hotels and restaurants to suit all budgets and tastes, organized by area, plus select nightlife listings, an alphabetical listing of practical information, and an overview of the best books and films to give you a flavor of the city.

Room with a view at the Fontainebleau

ACCOMMODATIONS

Miami has luxurious oceanfront resort hotels with restaurants run by star chefs, stylish and artsy boutique hotels, and of course its Art Deco hotel masterpieces. This may give the impression that accommodation is expensive, but that's far from the case. Naturally if you do want a 5-star hotel with ocean views you will pay highly for it. Move a few blocks back, though, and rates start to fall.

Miami is also a busy tourist city and many of the big US chains are found here, including both mid-range hotels and more budget motel-style accomodations. You may not be in the thick of the action but it certainly is worth investigating: check the location and transportation options, and you could save yourself a lot of money.

You also need to check the events calendar (see page 111) as prices during festivals and conventions rocket, but if you can be flexible on your dates and travel a week or two earlier or later, you'll find very different price ranges.

The same goes for choosing which season you travel in. High season means high prices, and you'll pay top dollars, but visit in the shoulder seasons and again, prices are much more affordable. Many of the hotels also have a very wide range of room rates, so don't write off those resort hotels and Art Deco classics. A smaller room in one of those places may be much better in terms of quality and value than a better room in a chain hotel. In short, before booking your trip to Miami you need to do some hotel homework.

Note that some of the tours have no hotel listings here, simply because there are few decent hotels in those more residential neighborhoods.

> Price for a standard double room for one night, excluding taxes and breakfast, in high season.
> $$$$ = over $250
> $$$ = $150-250
> $$ = $75-150
> $ = less than $75

Miami Beach

Fontainebleau Hilton Resort and Towers

4441 Collins Avenue; tel: 800-548-8886; www.fontainebleau.com; $$$$
This is an opulent and extensively renovated 1,206-room hotel built in the 1950s. Facilities include a pool with waterfalls, tennis courts, a health club, restaurants, nightclubs (with a famous Latin floorshow), shopping, and activities for children of all ages.

The National Hotel

1677 Collins Avenue; tel: 800-327-8370; www.nationalhotel.com; $$$

The pool area at The National Hotel

This is an elegant Art Deco landmark with all the amenities including a fitness room, massage, and a location right by the beach. It's beautifully renovated, and the long, narrow pool is both historic and unique.

The Richmond Hotel

1757 Collins Avenue; tel: 305-538-2331; www.richmondhotel.com; $$$

The Richmond is unusual in that it's still a family-run hotel, now in the third generation, which opened in 1941during the boom in Art Deco building. It has a beachfront location and its own pool, surrounded by palm trees.

The Sagamore Hotel

1671 Collins Avenue; tel: 305-535-8088; www.sagamorehotel.com; $$$$

The Sagamore is a luxury hotel in the Miami Beach Art Deco district, and has 93 suites, bungalows, and oceanfront penthouses. The décor is mostly minimalist chic, and amenities include a spa, pool, restaurant, and art collections in both public spaces and guest rooms.

Seagull Hotel Miami Beach

100 21st Street; tel: 305-538-6631; http://seagullhotelmiamibeach.com; $$$

This is one of the more affordable hotels in Miami Beach that boasts an oceanfront location with a white sand beach right in front of it. If you don't want to stroll to the beach there's also a pool and lush tropical gardens.

South Beach

The Cardozo Hotel

1300 Ocean Drive; tel: 800-782-6500; www.cardozohotel.com; $$$

This oceanfront Art Deco hotel may look familiar as it's featured in several movies. It was built in 1939 in the heart of the historic district of South Beach, with 44 rooms and suites, which were recently remodeled prior to a 2017 re-opening.

Clay Hotel

1438 Washington Avenue; tel: 800-379-CLAY; www.clayhotel.com; $-$$

This very popular 135-room hotel offers budget accommodation right in the Art Deco district of South Beach. There's a Mediterranean feel to the place, which has been here for over a century. Some rooms have balconies, and it's a five-minute walk to Ocean Drive.

The Clevelander Hotel

1020 Ocean Drive; tel: 305-532-4006; www.clevelander.com; $$$

If you want a lively hotel then the Clevelander is noted for its pool parties, with three bars located around the pool and patio area. There's also a sports bar inside, and they have live music or DJs most nights of the week.

Hotel Chelsea

944 Washington Avenue; tel: 305-534-4069; www.thehotelchelsea.com; $$

A hip hotel for the budget conscious, rooms here have stripped-down ele-

A suite at the Bal Harbour Quarzo

gance, with futon-style beds. A DJ plays in the lobby on weekends; the front patio overlooks the avenue. There's also a happy hour each night with complimentary drinks for guests.

Hotel St Augustine
347 Washington Avenue; tel: 800-310-7717; www.hotelstaugustine.com; $$$$
This 24-room boutique hotel oozes European chic in an Art Deco building in SoFi (South of Fifth), less than a five-minute walk to Ocean Drive and the waterfront. All rooms are soundproofed, non-smoking and have free WiFi.

Hotel Victor
1144 Ocean Drive; tel: 305-779-8700; http://hotelvictorsouthbeach.com; $$$$
The Victor is one of Miami's classic Art Deco hotels, but while the building is historic the vibe is definitely cool and modern. The rooms have wooden floors and iPod docks, there's a pool and a spa, and for overseas visitors the bonus of free international phone calls.

North Miami

Bal Harbour Quarzo
290 Bal Bay Drive, Bal Harbour; tel: 305-222-7922; www.quarzohotel.com/miami-luxury-hotels; $$$$
One of the best luxury hotels in Miami, the Bal Harbour Quarzo also boasts a great location overlooking the intracoastal waterway. The rooms and suites have are exquisite, and you can book in-room or garden massages. There's an outdoor pool too.

Daddy O Hotel
9660 E. Bay Harbor Drive; tel: 305-868-4141; www.daddyohotel.com/miami; $$–$$$
This chic waterfront boutique hotel in Bay Harbor Islands features in-room iPod docks and flat-screen TVs, as well as designer furniture. There's a business center, passes to the nearby LA Fitness gym, and room service from the adjoining Palm Restaurant.

Wynwood

Midtown Inn Miami
3400 Biscayne Blvd; tel: 305-573-7700; www.midtowninnmiami.com; $$
Accommodation is limited in Wynwood but the nearby Midtown Inn is an affordable option. The 36 rooms are simple but clean, and there's an outdoor pool. There's no restaurant but numerous eating options are within a few minutes' walk.

Downtown Miami

Hyatt Regency Miami
400 SE 2nd Avenue: tel: 305-358-1234; https://miami.regency.hyatt.com; $$$
The Hyatt has 615 non-smoking rooms and suites, some with views over the bay or the Miami River. It has an outdoor pool and a 24-hour gym, while dining options include the Riverwalk Café, Riverwalk Deli, and the Pure Verde Lounge serving Miami/Latin food and drinks.

The Mandarin Oriental enjoys a glorious setting

InterContinental

100 Chopin Plaza; tel: 800-327-3005;
www.icmiamihotel.com;
$$$$

This soaring, high-rise hotel has 639 rooms, several gourmet restaurants, a rooftop pool with views over the city and Biscayne Bay, access to a 24-hour fitness center, and a jogging track, all in the center of Downtown Miami.

Kimpton EPIC Hotel

270 Biscayne Blvd Way; tel: 305-424-5226;
www.epichotel.com; $$$$

This modern 4-star hotel has a spa and two pools, and there's a complimentary wine hour daily from 5–6pm. There are also fantastic views from the Area 31 restaurant on the 16th floor.

Leamington Hotel

307 North East 1st Street; tel: 305-373-7783; www.leamingtonhotel.com;
$$

The Leamington offers good value-for-money for a Downtown hotel. The 82 rooms are basic but comfortable, all with en-suite facilities, and there's a complimentary breakfast. It also offers a limited number of free airport shuttles during the day.

JW Marriott Marquis Miami

255 Biscayne Blvd Way; tel: 305-421-8600;
www.marriott.com/hotels/travel/miamj-jw-marriott-marquis-miami; $$$–$$$$

The Marriott offers 5-star luxury in Downtown Miami, with 313 rooms and suites, some with views out over the water. It has a spa and fitness center (offering free classes), and the Db Bistro Moderne is a highly-acclaimed restaurant.

Miami Sun Hotel

226 NE 1st Avenue; tel: 305-375-0786;
www.themiamisunhotel.com; $$

The Miami Sun has been providing budget accommodation here since the 1920s. Rooms are simple but clean, and there's a complimentary breakfast and free WiFi. It's a seven-minute walk to the Bayside Marketplace.

The Bay

Mandarin Oriental Miami

500 Brickell Key Drive; tel: 305-913-8288;
www.mandarinoriental.com/miami;
$$$$

On the southern tip of Brickell Key, overlooking Brickell Key Park and the bay, the 5-star Mandarin Oriental has rooms and suites with amazing views. There's also a spa, an infinity pool, and a choice of bars and gourmet restaurants.

Brickell

Aloft Miami – Brickell

1001 SW 2nd Avenue; tel: 305-854-6300;
www.aloftmiamibrickell.com; $$–$$$

Aloft is a very design-conscious hotel whose amenities include the W XYZ Bar, a fashionable meeting place which offers live music and DJs, seasonal cocktails, wine, beer, and a snacks menu. There's also a gym and pool.

The pool at the Sonesta Coconut Grove

Fortune House Hotel

185 Southeast 14th Terrace #102; tel: 305-349-5200; www.fortunehousehotel. com; $$$$

This modern hotel is a short stroll from the waterfront. Its range of rooms and suites have either water or city views, and are equipped with kitchens, washers, and dryers for longer-stay guests. Some rooms are available at cheaper rates.

SLS Brickell

1300 S Miami Avenue; tel: 305-239-1300; http://slshotels.com/brickell; $$$$

The Brickell outpost of the intimate and artsy SLS chain of hotels is designed by Philippe Starck and has a rooftop pool deck and a spa. It has two restaurants, one run by a James Beard Award-winning chef, and 124 rooms and suites.

Hotel Urbano

2500 Brickell Avenue, tel: 305-854-2070; www.hotelurbanomiami.com; $$$

Located right by the causeway that links Virginia Key to the mainland, the Urbano boasts a sophisticated décor where the walls are covered with works by local artists. There's an outdoor pool with a fire pit, a fitness center and a lounge bar serving complimentary breakfast.

Virginia Key and Key Biscayne

The Ritz-Carlton Key Biscayne

455 Grand Bay Drive, Key Biscayne; tel: 305-365-4500; www.ritzcarlton.com/en/ hotels/miami/key-biscayne; $$$$

This resort hotel offers all the top-notch quality you would expect from the Ritz-Carlton name, with access to miles of beaches, and amenities including separate children and adult pools, a spa, a fitness center, tennis courts, and a range of eating options including oceanfront dining.

Coconut Grove

Mayfair Hotel and Spa

3000 Florida Avenue; tel: 305-441-0000; www.mayfairhotelandspa.com; $$$

The Mayfair is a stylish 4-star hotel only a five-minute walk from Coconut Grove's waterfront parks and is an intriguing mix of Art Deco, art nouveau and Caribbean-style décor. It has 179 suites with private balconies, and most suites also have their own hot tubs.

The Mutiny Hotel

2951 South Bayshore Drive; tel: 305-441-2100; www.providentresorts.com/mutiny-hotel; $$$

Overlooking Bayside Park and a couple of minutes' stroll to Biscayne Bay, this all-suites hotel has a stylish modern design, its own restaurant, a pool, spa, fitness center, sauna and steam room. It's also only a five-minute walk from the CocoWalk shopping and entertainment center.

Residence Inn by Marriott Miami Coconut Grove

2835 Tigertail Avenue; tel: 305-285-9303; www.marriott.com/hotels/travel/miaco-

The Caribbean-style Hawk's Cay Resort

residence-inn-miami-coconut-grove; $$$

Only a five-minute walk from Bayside, this all-suites hotel has two outdoor pools, a fitness center, and a complimentary breakfast. The suites all have kitchens, making it ideal if you want to self-cater.

Sonesta Coconut Grove

2889 McFarlane Road; tel: 305-529-2828; www.sonesta.com/us/florida/miami/sonesta-coconut-grove-miami; $$$

The Sonesta is close to Biscayne Bay and its pool and lounge offer great ocean views. It also has a restaurant serving Latin American cuisine, a fitness center, business center, and even two squash courts on the 8th floor. Ask for a Bay View room.

Florida Keys

Cypress House

601 Caroline Street, Key West; tel: 800-525-2488; www.historickeywestinns.com/the-inns/cypress-house/; $$$–$$$$

This elegant but unpretentious 1895 adults-only B&B is a fine example of Bahamian architecture. Rooms in the inn and in two nearby historic buildings are well appointed, with TVs and air conditioning; two on the first floor share a bath. The continental breakfast buffet is plentiful and afternoon cocktails are served by the secluded pool.

Dove Creek Lodge

147 Seaside Avenue (MM 94.5), Key Largo; tel: 305-852-6200; www.dovecreeklodge.com; $$$$

The emphasis at this refined waterfront lodge is on service. Rooms are large, with balconies, DVD players, large-screen TVs, and Internet. Staff can arrange a variety of activities, including deep-sea fishing.

Hawk's Cay Resort

61 Hawks Cay Boulevard, Duck Key; tel: 800-395-5539; www.hawkscay.com; $$$

This is a rambling Caribbean-style resort that pampers guests, with 176 rooms, swimming pool, tennis courts, restaurants, bars, boat rental, and scuba lessons. Duck Key is about halfway between Key Largo and Key West, so a perfect stopping point to break the journey.

Island City House Hotel

411 William Street, Key West; tel: 800-634-8230; www.islandcityhouse.com; $$$

Off the main strip, the Island City House Hotel has a tropical garden with 24 suites, most with kitchens and whirlpool tubs. There is a swimming pool, too.

Jules Undersea Lodge

51 Shoreland Drive (MM 103.2), Key Largo; tel: 305-451-2353; www.jul.com; $$$

Experience underwater living in this extraordinary subaquatic hotel, billed as the world's only underwater hotel. It's located right in the lagoon of the Key Largo Undersea Park, and you can combine your stay with a scuba diving course.

Joe's Stone Crab's claws

RESTAURANTS

Thanks to its diverse cultures, Miami has a dining scene that's exciting and varied. There's a lot of fusion going on, whether it be Caribbean-American, French-American, Asian-Mediterranean, or any other combination you can think of. The area's fresh seafood can be served plain and simple or spiced up with Cuban flavors, or turned into exquisite sushi by the multinational chefs who work here.

Miami is also broad in terms of price-ranges too. It can support high-end restaurants, mid-range bistros and wine bars, or fun places in artsy settings, down to basic places like pizza restaurants or Cuban street food. A number of top restaurants do fixed-price lunch menus, where you might be able to choose between three or four courses and try food from the best chefs without racking up a huge bill. Sampler pates, whether of Cuban food or seafood, are also a great way to expand your culinary experience.

There are one or two things to remember: it's common practice in Miami to add a tip to a bill automatically, so always check your bill before paying to see if you're happy with the suggested level of tip, and to avoid tipping twice. Also, in Miami people tend to eat later than they do in many places in the US: dinner at 8pm, say, rather than from 5–6pm. If you don't mind eating early, it can be one way to get a table at restaurants that otherwise get booked up.

Miami Beach

The Forge
432 41st Street; tel: 305-538-8533; www.theforge.com; daily D; $$$$
An institution in Miami Beach since 1968, it is a magnet for celebrities and celeb-spotters. Tuxedoed servers give tours of the historic and well-stocked wine cellar. Steaks are the best but they cater for vegetarians and vegans too.

Hakkasan
Fontainebleau Hotel, 4441 Collins Avenue; tel: 877-326-7412; http://hakkasan.com/locations/hakkasan-miami; daily D, Sat–Sun L; $$$$
This was the first US location for the international Hakkasan chain of contemporary Cantonese restaurants, and it's earned an AAA Four-Diamond rating. The cool lighting and subtle Oriental-style décor complement dishes such as spicy Szechuan chicken or pan-fried Wagyu beef.

Price for a two-course meal for one including a glass of wine (or other beverage)
$$$$ = over $60
$$$ = $45-60
$$ = $20-45
$ = under $20

Nobu Miami

Eden Roc Hotel, 4525 Collins Avenue; tel: 305-695-3232; www.noburestaurants.com/miami; daily D; $$–$$$

The fixed-price menus at lunchtime in the lobby bar are a good way to sample some of the best Japanese food in the city without breaking the bank. Or come here for dinner to try one of their classic dishes like pan-seared scallops with jalapeno salsa.

Yuca

501 Lincoln Road; tel: 305-532-9822; www.yuca.com; daily L and D; $$

Yuca stands for Young Urban Cuban American, which says a lot about the vibe and the food. The lunch menu is more casual, with sandwiches, burgers, and soups, but for dinner you can enjoy starters such as Cuban calamari and mains including *ceviche* or Cuban tacos.

South Beach

Joe's Stone Crab

11 Washington Avenue; tel: 305-673-0365; www.joesstonecrab.com; Wed–Sun D; $$$$

The oldest and most talked about restaurant on the beach, Joe's is great if you can nab a table (no reservations). Service is brusque but worth it for the stone crabs, in season from mid-Oct through mid-May. The restaurant is closed Aug–Sep.

Poseidon

1131 Washington Avenue; tel: 305-534-4434; http://poseidonmiami.com; daily L and D; $$

This Greek restaurant and outdoor lounge imports many of its herbs, spices, and oils from Greece. All the Greek classics are here plus a few less common dishes too, such as chicken artichoke and *calamari saganaki*.

Spiga

Impala Hotel, 1228 Collins Avenue; tel: 305-534-0079; www.spigarestaurant.com; daily D; $$$

Winner of numerous accolades Spiga is one of the best Italian restaurants in town. They make their own pasta fresh every morning and the pasta-seafood combinations, the fresh baby clams especially, are real winners.

Tap Tap

819 5th Street; tel: 305-672-2898; www.taptapsouthbeach.com; daily L and D; $$

The only Haitian eatery on the beach, this Caribbean restaurant is decorated with brightly colored murals. The food, including fried pork tidbits and curried goat stew, recalls the taste of the islands. Live music on weekends completes the scene.

Toni's Sushi Bar

1208 Washington Avenue; tel: 305-673-9368; www.tonisushi.com; daily D; $$$

This was the first Japanese restaurant in Miami Beach when it opened in 1987, and still pleases lovers of raw fish with superb sushi served in cosy curtained booths. It's usually crowded on weekends, but worth the wait.

Guava pastelitos at Versailles

North Miami

L'Auberge

13315 W. Dixie Highway; tel: 305-891-0077; no website; daily B, L and D; $$

This Haitian eatery (Haiti's two national languages are French and Haitian Creole, hence the French name) may look nothing from the outside but the food is excellent and authentic and you'll hear customers speaking Creole. Try fried fish with fried plantains, fried chicken, fish soup, or *piklis* (a spicy cabbage salad).

Steve's Pizza

12101 Biscayne Blvd; tel: 305-891-0202; no website; daily L and D; $

Steve's is the kind of hole-in-the-wall place that visitors would walk right by if not for the lines of locals queuing up for its authentic New York-style pizza.

Wynwood

Michael's Genuine Food & Drink

130 NE 40th Street; tel: 305-573-5550; http://michaelsgenuine.com; daily L and D; $$$

On the edge of Wynwood in the Design District, this casual place has a James Beard Award-winning chef and a daily-changing menu. There's a raw oyster bar and inventive dishes like Rock Shrimp and Chorizo Pizza.

Plant Food + Wine

105 NE 24th Street; tel: 305-814-5365; https://matthewkenneycuisine.com/hospitality/plantfoodandwinemiami; daily L and D; $$$

One of a small chain of restaurants run by chef Matthew Kenney, this place proves that vegan food can also be gourmet. There's a chef's tasting menu, or individual dishes such as coconut ceviche tacos.

Wynwood Kitchen & Bar

2550 NW 2nd Avenue; tel: 305-722-8959; www.wynwoodkitchenandbar.com; daily L, Mon–Sat D; $$

Hip joint with bold modern artworks on the walls serving quality but affordable American classics like burgers and ribs and their skewers of pork belly or baby octopus are also fantastically tasty.

Overtown

Casablanca Seafood Bar and Grill

400 North River Drive; tel: 305-371-4107; www.casablancaseafood.com; daily B, L and D; $$$

"Boat to table" is the motto here and this smart seafood place does indeed have its own fish market next door, and waterfront views too. You could start with oysters from the raw bar, indulge in a whole stuffed lobster, or have something simpler like a grouper sandwich or even steak.

CRUST

668 NW 5th Street; tel: 305-371-7065; www.crust-usa.com; Tue–Sun D; $$

This casual Italian place near the river looks nothing from the outside but inside you'll find a great atmosphere and an extensive pizza menu (grilled

The slick Azul restaurant at the Mandarin Oriental

octopus being one of their more unusual toppings on offer) alongside pasta, soups, salads, sandwiches, and mains like chicken parmesan.

La Carreta

3632 SW 8th Street; tel: 305-444-7501; http://lacarreta.com; daily B, L and D; $$

There are several branches of La Carreta around the city all serving similar menus in a lively setting with Cuban specialties such as *picadillo*, *ropa vieja*, and *boliche*, though a Cuban sampler plate is a good idea for novices.

Versailles Restaurant

3555 SW 8th Street; tel: 305-444-0240; www.versaillesrestaurant.com; daily B, L and D; $$

Versailles has been serving up tasty Cuban food since 1971, and its ornate interior is indeed reminiscent of the French palace's lavish Galerie des Glaces. Check their daily specials as well as regular menu items like chicken and yellow rice or Cuban-style pot roast.

Downtown Miami

Db Bistro Moderne

JW Marriott Marquis Miami, 255 Biscayne Blvd Way; tel: 305-421-8800; www.dbbistro.com/miami; Mon–Fri L, Mon–Sat D; $$$$

Chef Daniel Boulud serves creative French-American cuisine at one of the best restaurants in town. Smart-casual is the feel, and the fixed-price lunch is a bargain. Otherwise try black truffle risotto or the original db burger, also with black truffles.

CVI.CHE 105

105 NE 3rd Avenue; tel: 305-577-3454; http://ceviche105.com/downtownmiami; daily L and D; $$

You know from the name that this Peruvian place is going to be a hip hangout, but it's also been voted best Downtown restaurant several times, along with many other accolades. Try one of their *ceviches*, see if you agree.

Zuma

EPIC Hotel, 270 Biscayne Blvd Way; tel: 305-577-0277; www.zumarestaurant.com; daily L and D; $$$$

Miami's branch of an international chain serves up contemporary Japanese food with more than a few twists. The riverside terrace is the perfect spot for dishes such as spicy beef tenderloin with sesame, red chili, and sweet soy.

The Bay

Azul

Mandarin Oriental, 500 Brickell Key Drive; tel: 305-913-8358; www.mandarinoriental.com/miami/fine-dining/azul; Tue–Sat D; $$$$

With views over Biscayne Bay and the city skyline through floor-to-ceiling windows, Azul is hard to beat for location. Its classy style is the perfect setting for the fusion of Asian and Mediterranean cuisine that makes it one of the city's top restaurants.

The award-winning Palme d'Or

NIU Kitchen

134 NE 2nd Avenue; tel: 786-542-5050;
www.niukitchen.com; Mon–Sat L; daily D; $$
If you like tapas then definitely give this
casual country-style Spanish place a try.
You can order individual plates, com-
bos, and there are sandwiches and full
plates as well, including steaks, ribs, or
the catch of the day.

Brickell

The Capital Grille

444 Brickell Avenue; tel: 305-374-4500;
www.thecapitalgrille.com/locations/fl/miami/
miami/8006; Mon–Fri L, daily D; $$$$
This may be one of a big chain of steak-
houses but it's classy and still delivers
the goods at its Brickell branch. You
can get seafood and other meats but
dishes like porterhouse steak or a 22 oz
bone-in ribeye are hard to beat.

Perricone's

15 SE 10th Street; tel: 305-374-9449;
www.perricones.com; daily L and D,
Sat–Sun B; $$$
This long-running and always busy Italian
place is shaded by palms and other trees
and has garden as well as indoor dining. It also has its own market and deli,
with daily deli specials, and it's won rave
reviews for dishes such as baked brie en
croûte and homemade potato gnocchi.

The River Seafood Oyster Bar

650 S Miami Avenue; tel: 305-530-1915;
www.therivermiami.com; Mon–Fri L, daily
D; $$$

This club-like place with its piano bar is a
place for a special occasion with classy
service and mouthwatering dishes like
Coconut-Steamed Mussels, Octopus
Salad, or Curried Fisherman's Stew.

Virginia Key and Key Biscayne

The Rusty Pelican

201 Rickenbacker Causeway, Key Biscayne;
tel: 305-361-3838; www.therustypelican.
com; daily L and D; $$$
This casual waterfront restaurant has
wonderful views back across the bay
to Miami. Its menu ranges from sushi
to steaks but it's noted for its seafood,
with oysters and clams as starters, and
bacon-wrapped scallops making for a
mouthwatering main course.

Coconut Grove

Le Bouchon

3430 Main Highway; tel: 305-448-6060;
http://lebouchondugrove.com; daily B, L
and D; $$–$$$
This French bistro definitely has the
French theme covered. Starters include
traditional escargots and foie gras, with
mains such as a French red wine beef
stew or home-made duck leg confit.

Greenstreet Café

3468 Main Highway; tel: 305-444-0244;
www.greenstreetcafe.net; daily B, L and
D; $$
This very popular neighborhood place
is as much community hangout as eat-
ing place, but the food is excellent. It's

a great place for breakfast, and they make all their own bread and pastries every day.

Lulu in the Grove

3105 Commodore Plaza; tel: 305-447-5858; http://luluinthegrove.com; Sat–Sun B, daily L and D; $$
Try to grab a sidewalk table at this smart place. Its wide-ranging menu means you can eat a little or a lot. The pasta and salads are good, though you can also enjoy burgers and steaks, while their fish tacos are a treat.

Palme d'Or at The Biltmore Hotel

1200 Anastasia Avenue; tel: 305-913-3200; www.biltmorehotel.com/dining/palme_dor.php; Tue–Sat D; $$$$
This is a little outside Coconut Grove in Coral Gables, but worth including as it's been rated as the best restaurant in Florida. It's a classic formal place, so dress your best and consider the ultimate treat, the 11-course Chef's Tasting Menu.

The Florida Keys

A&B Lobster House

700 Front St, Key West; tel: 305-294-5880; http://aandblobsterhouse.com; daily D; $$$–$$$$
The caviar is delivered fresh daily, and lobsters are flown in from Maine. House specialties include grouper Oscar, Brazil nut snapper, and farm-raised baby conch sautéed in rum butter sauce. The waterfront view is spectacular from the wrap-around balcony.

Ballyhoo's Island Grille

97860 Overseas Hwy (MM 97.8 Median), Key Largo; tel: 305-852-0822; www.ballyhoosrestaurant.com; daily L and D; $
Although it's right on Route 1, this venerable restaurant in a 1930s conch house was once part of a fishing camp and there is definitely a feeling of stepping back in time. The all-you-can-eat fish and stone crab claw specials can't be beat.

B.O.'s Fish Wagon

801 Caroline St, Key West; tel: 305-294-9272; www.bosfishwagon.com; daily L and D; $
Many consider this rustic, open-air spot to be a defining Key West dining experience. Get in line for delicious, if somewhat pricy, fish sandwiches, chili, conch fritters, and home-made fries. Live entertainment makes the evenings a pleasure. No credit cards.

The Fish House

102401 Overseas Hwy (MM 102.4), Key Largo; tel: 305-451-4665; www.thefishhouse.com; daily L and D; $–$$
Fresh fish is delivered right to the kitchen door and filleted on the spot at this conch-style eatery which specializes in… fish. That said their curly-topped key lime pie is a slice of heaven. Next door, the Fish House Encore has a sushi bar, all-you-can-eat specials, and piano music weekend evenings.

NIGHTLIFE

Miami is one of the best places in Florida for nightlife. Bars and nightclubs abound, whether you're looking for gay-friendly venues, salsa music, southern sounds, or all three. Then there are numerous casinos to tempt you and movie theaters for a more sedate night out.

Miami is also the base for cultural institutions, such as the Florida Grand Opera, Miami City Ballet and the New World Symphony Orchestra. There are also many universities and colleges around the city, and they too host public performances.

Casinos

Casino Miami
3500 NW 37th Avenue, Miami; tel: 305-633-6400; www.casinomiamijaialai.com
One of the city's newer casinos, with the latest slot machines, an area for electronic table games, sports betting and live jai alai games. There's also a restaurant, the Club Rio entertainment venue, and a Whiskies Bar with cheap drinks.

Hialeah Casino
100 E 32nd St, Hialeah; tel: 305- 885-8000; http://hialeahparkcasino.com
The casino was added to the historic Hialeah Park Race Track in 2013. It has almost 900 slots, a stylish 33-table Poker Room, electronic table games, and of course the chance to take in some racing and enjoy the race track's restaurants, bars and live entertainment.

Magic City Casino
450 NW 37th Avenue, Miami; tel: 305-649-3000; www.magiccitycasino.com
Magic City is one of the longest established casinos in town and has over 800 slots, 19 tables in the Poker Room, greyhound racing at the 80-year-old Flagler Dog Track from June to October, a restaurant and buffet, a bar and lounge, and live entertainment.

Cinemas

Bill Cosford Cinema
5030 Brunson Drive, Coral Gables; tel: Programming/Scheduling 305-284-9838, Box Office 305-284-4627; www.cosfordcinema.com
This single-screen art-house cinema on the University of Miami campus has been in existence for 60 years, and moviemakers such as Jon Landis and Kevin Spacey have come here to talk about their films.

Cinépolis Coconut Grove
CocoWalk, 3015 Grand Ave, Miami; tel: 305-446-6843; http://cinepolisusa.com/coconut-grove.aspx
Home to the Miami International Film Festival, this multi-screen cinema with reserved seating is one for the indulgent and social movie experience. It has a bar and lounge with beer and wine, and you can take your snacks and drinks in with you into four of the screens, which have leather chairs with swivel tray tables.

The well-established Bill Cosford Cinema

Coral Gables Art Cinema

260 Aragon Ave, Coral Gables; tel: 786-472-2249; www.gablescinema.com

If you prefer independent movies and foreign films then this is one of the biggest and most comfortable art cinemas in southern Florida. They screen classic revivals too, as well as special events like late-night seasons, or themed seasons like 20th-Century Women.

Miami Beach Cinematheque

1130 Washington Ave, Miami Beach; tel: 305-673-4567; http://mbcinema.com

Small and quirky cinema designed like someone's living room, with stripped wood flooring, bookshelves, and prints on the walls. Based in the 1927 City Hall it is home to the Miami Beach Film Society, so expect a quality arthouse program. There's also a café, a bookstore/library, and an art gallery.

O Cinema Wynwood

90 NW 29th St, Miami; tel: 305-571-9970; www.o-cinema.org/venue/o-cinema-wynwood

With its front-row sofas and cheap prices, this is one of the most popular independent cinemas, showing indie, foreign, and family-friendly films as well as classic revivals. It has a café and bar. Also branches in Miami Shores and North Beach.

Tower Theater Miami

1508 SW 8th St, Miami; tel: 305-643-8706; www.towertheatermiami.com

This unique cinema in Little Havana was the biggest state-of-the-art theater in the South when it opened in 1926. Despite its grandeur it keeps its prices cheap, and it also has a number of free showings.

Live Music Venues

AmericanAirlines Arena

601 Biscayne Blvd, Miami; tel: 786-777-1000; www.aaarena.com

This is Miami's main music and sports venue where the big-name acts play. It's also home to the Miami Heat basketball team and has hosted several NBA Finals.

Ball and Chain

1513 SW 8th St, Miami; tel: 305-643-7820; https://ballandchainmiami.com

This classic venue in Little Havana was a nightclub from 1935 through to the 1950s, attracting performers like Billie Holliday, but today it hosts some of the best live Latin American music around. Watch out for the Sunday afternoon shows too.

Bardot

3456 N Miami Ave, Miami; tel: 305-576-5570; http://bardotmiami.com

Bardot is a well-known and very cool Miami lounge with a mix of live music and DJs, and a mix of styles from electronic through to acoustic singer-songwriter, so be sure to check the program. Allow a little time to find the unmarked entrance, too. Affordable but inventive cocktail list, and front-of-stage sofa seating are big draws.

Churchill's Pub

5501 NE 2nd Avenue, Miami; tel: 305-757-1807; www.churchillspub.com

The pineapple stage in the back courtyard at Ball and Chain

This legendary Little Haiti bar has been going strong since 1979. The Monday night Miami Jazz jam features pretty much every style of music on its calendar, with live music every night of the week. It's a great showcase for local bands but also the kind of place where big names might do a secret gig when they're in town.

Gramps Bar and Music

176 NW 24th St, Miami; tel: 305-699-2669; www.gramps.com

This fashionable bar and music venue hosts live acts and DJs, but comedy also features high. There's patio dining outside and air-conditioning inside.

Hoy Como Ayer

2212 SW 8th St, Miami; tel: 305-541-2631; tel: www.hoycomoayer.us

One of the best places in Little Havana to hear authentic Cuban music 'Today as yesterday' lives up to its name with eclectic music from traditional styles to modern rock and pop. There is food from a simple menu, but it's a small place so go early.

Klipsch Amphitheater at Bayfront Park

301 Biscayne Blvd, Miami; tel: 305-358-7550; www.klipsch.com/klipsch-amphitheater-at-bayfront-park

This waterfront auditorium seating 7,500 is the perfect venue on a fine Miami day or evening. The concerts are only occasional events but worth watching out for. Past acts include Robert Plant, John Legend, the Marley Brothers, and Maroon 5.

Lagniappe

3425 NE 2nd Ave, Miami; tel: 305-576-0108; www.lagniappehouse.com

This no-reservations, New Orleans-style restaurant and wine bar hosts live music at 9pm every night, from bluegrass to jazz to Latin American.

Mango's Tropical Café

900 Ocean Drive, Miami Beach; tel: 305-673-4422; www.mangos.com/miami

A Miami institution, it appeals more to visitors than locals but is a terrific night out. The location is right by the water, and the décor is Haitian. The rest is a mix of Caribbean and Latin American – the food, the cocktails, the showgirls, and the music.

Nightclubs

The Electric Pickle

2826 N Miami Ave, Miami; tel: 305-456-5613; http://electricpicklemiami.com

This place is geared to live music and club dance events, doing them both really well.

LIV@Fontainebleau Miami Beach

Fontainebleau Miami Beach, 4441 Collins Ave, Miami Beach; tel: 305-674-4680; www.livnightclub.com

Voted one of the best clubs in the world, if you only go to one club in Miami, make it this one. The interior is spectacular and attracts VIPs and the beautiful people.

Mynt Lounge

1921 Collins Ave, Miami Beach; tel: 305-532-0727; www.myntlounge.com/web

Go to Hoy Como Ayer for authentic Cuban music and mojitos

This vast club has an Ultra Lounge for celebs and VIPs only. Dress your best if you hope to get through the door to enjoy the DJs, the hip-hop, and the go-go dancers.

STORY Nightclub

136 Collins Ave, Miami Beach; tel: 305-479-4426; http://storymiami.com
One of the best nightclubs in the city, STORY has five bars, VIP tables, state-of-the-art sound, a big dance floor, bottle service, and a reputation for attracting both the newest and the best DJs.

Twist

1057 Washington Ave, Miami Beach; tel: 305-538-9478; www.twistsobe.com
Twist is one of the best gay clubs in Miami with seven bars spread over two levels as well as DJs and drag queens.

Theaters and Performing Arts

Adrienne Arsht Center for the Performing Arts

1300 Biscayne Blvd, Miami; tel: 305-949-6722; www.arshtcenter.org
The second-biggest performing arts center in the US after New York's Lincoln Center, it's the home of the Miami City Ballet, the Florida Grand Opera and hosts a range of music, drama, comedy, and other genres.

Colony Theater

Lincoln Rd Mall, 1040 Lincoln Rd, Miami Beach; tel: 1-800-211-1414; www.colonymb.org
First opened in 1935 as a cinema, this restored Art Deco gem is a superb venue for the resident Miami New Drama group.

Fillmore Miami Beach at the Jackie Gleason Theater

1700 Washington Ave, Miami Beach; tel: 305-673-7300; www.fillmoremb.com
Artists such as Tony Bennett and Sting have performed here, and this Art Deco venue also features comedy and drama.

New World Center

500 17th St, Miami Beach; tel: 305-673-3330; www.nws.edu
Designed by Frank Gehry, this is the home for Miami's New World Symphony and features dance and classical music concerts.

Olympia Theater

174 E Flagler St, Miami; tel: 305-374-2444; www.olympiatheater.org
This historic venue opened in 1926 and has hosted The Marx Brothers and BB King. There are free events every Wednesday evening in the Lobby Lounge, as well as drama and movie shows.

South Miami–Dade Cultural Arts Center

10950 SW 211 St, Miami; tel: 786-573-5316; www.smdcac.org
Contemporary arts of all sorts – dance, comedy, drama, food trucks, festivals, kids shows, visiting artists, and more.

Waterfront Theater

601 Biscayne Blvd, Miami; tel: 786-777-1000; www.aaarena.com
In the AmericanAirlines Arena, the largest theater in Florida seats up to 5,800 people for concerts, musicals and family events.

Miami Beach policemen

A–Z

A

Age Restrictions

The minimum age of consent in Florida is 18. You must be 21 to buy or drink alcohol, and 16 to drive.

B

Budgeting

Miami is relatively expensive and you can expect to pay $5–8 for a pint of beer, although happy hours can halve that price. Budget for about $7 upwards for a glass of wine. A main course at a budget or fast food restaurant is about $8, at a moderate restaurant it would be about $10–15, and at more expensive places expect to pay $25 upwards. For a cheap hotel budget about $50–100 for a room. Make that $100–200 for a moderate hotel and $250–500 for a more expensive place.

A taxi from the airport should cost about $35–45. A single bus or Metro-rail ticket valid for up to three hours and including a bus-to-bus transfer costs $2.25. A 1-day pass costs $5.65 and a 7-day pass is $29.25. Go Miami cards are available which include the Hop-On-Hop-Off bus and admission to 25+ attractions, but not public transportation. Costs range from $69 for a 1-day adult card ($59 for children aged 3–12) to $182 for a 5-day card ($150 for children). There are also 2-day and 3-day options at $105/$85 and $136/$115 respectively.

C

Children

Although it's a long way from the theme parks of Orlando, Miami is still a child-friendly place and a popular family holiday destination. There are plenty of attractions and activities suitable for the whole family. Many of the resort hotels have special programs for children, and baby-sitting options when it's time for the parents to have fun.

Clothing

For most of the year you'll want to pack lightly and casually, perhaps with one or two smarter outfits if you plan to visit any high-end restaurants. Mostly, though, shorts and t-shirts will be fine, with jeans and casual shirts for chillier days and cooler evenings, even in winter. Winter's also the dry season, but the rest of the year you should pack an umbrella, just in case.

Crime and Safety

Florida as a whole doesn't have a squeaky-clean reputation when it comes to crime, and attacks committed against tourists ruin the state's idyllic vacation-in-the-sun image periodically. The

authorities have come up with various safeguards designed to protect visitors. Many of these are aimed at motorists, particularly in Miami, where a number of violent assaults have occurred when jet-lagged tourists disembarked long flights, missed the highway signs for Miami Beach, and found themselves in high-crime areas.

Car rental agencies have removed the special license plates that made rental cars an easy mark and have replaced them with standard-issue plates used by residents. In Miami, road signs have been improved and orange sunburst signs help guide visiting drivers along the main routes to and from the airport.

A little common sense goes a long way: don't carry large sums of money or expensive video/camera equipment, don't wear expensive or expensive-looking jewelry, and don't flaunt your new smartphone. Walk purposefully and don't make eye contact with unwelcome strangers or respond to come-ons. Don't travel alone at night. Keep valuables in the room safe, if you have one, and ask the staff in your hotel for advice about areas that should be avoided. All that said, the crime rate in Florida is at its lowest for 45 years, and the overwhelming majority of people will have a trouble-free vacation in Miami.

Customs

You can bring into the US the following duty-free items: 1 liter of alcohol, if over 21 years of age; 200 cigarettes, 50 cigars (not Cuban) or 2kg of tobacco, if you're over 18; and gifts worth up to $100 ($800 for US citizens). Travelers with more than $10,000 in US or foreign currency, travelers checks, or money orders must declare these upon entry. Meats, fruits, vegetables, seeds, or plants (and many prepared foods made from them) cannot be brought in to the country and must be disposed of in the bins provided before entering. For more information, contact US Customs & Border Protection (tel: 877-227-5511; www.cbp.gov).

Disabled Travelers

From ADA-compliant hotels to on-loan beach chairs and even mobility-assisted snorkeling and hang-gliding, visitor services throughout Miami and Florida go to great lengths to make sure everyone enjoys barrier-free access to sun and fun.

Under the Americans with Disabilities Act (ADA), accommodations built after January 26, 1995, and containing more than five rooms must be usable by persons with disabilities. Older and smaller inns and lodges are often wheelchair-accessible. For the sight-impaired, many hotels provide special alarm clocks, captioned television services, and security measures. To comply with ADA hearing-impaired requirements, hotels have begun to

The Miami Gay Pride

follow special procedures; local agencies may provide TTY and interpretation services. Check with the front desk when you make reservations to ascertain to what degree the hotel complies with ADA guidelines. Ask specific questions regarding bathroom facilities, bed height, wheelchair space, and availability of services.

Restaurants and attractions are required to build ramps for those with limited mobility. Many major attractions have wheelchairs for loan or rent. Some provide menus, visitor guides, and interpreters for hearing- and seeing-impaired guests.

You can hire a wheelchair-accessible taxi from several companies including Crown Taxi (305-445-5555) and Comfort Wheelchair Transportation (305-532-5555).

All public buses are now wheelchair-accessible, with reduced fares in place. For more information on public services for disabled travelers visit the Miami–Dade County government website: www.miamidade.gov/Portal_Content/government/disabilities.asp.

For more information, read Wheelchairs on the Go: Accessible Fun in Florida by Michelle Stigleman and Deborah Van Brunt. For disability resources in Florida, contact the Clearinghouse on Disability (tel: 850-497-3423 or 877-232-4968). The Society for the Advancement of Travel for the Handicapped (tel: 212-447-7284; www.sath.org) publishes a quarterly magazine.

E

Electricity

The United States uses 110–120 volts AC (60 cycles). If visiting from outside North America, you may require an electrical adapter with two flat pins for any electronics or appliances you want to bring. You won't need a transformer.

Embassies and Consulates

Foreign embassies are all located in Washington, DC, with several consulates in or near Miami, including:

Australia: Consulate General of Australia, 251 Buttonwood Drive, Key Biscayne, FL 33149; tel: 305-519-8814.

Canada: Consulate General of Canada, 200 South Biscayne Blvd., Suite 1600, Miami, FL 33131; tel: 305-579-1600; www.miami.gc.ca.

Ireland: Consulate General of Ireland, 400 Fifth Avenue South, Suite 301, Naples, FL 34102; tel: 239-649-1001.

UK: Consulate General of United Kingdom, 1001 Brickell Bay Drive, Suite 2800, Miami, Florida 33131; tel: 305-374-1522.

Emergencies

Wherever you are in Miami or the rest of Florida, in case of emergency dial 911 to contact the local police, fire, or ambulance service.

Etiquette

Miami is a very relaxed and multina-

Calle Ocho street festival

tional city, with casual clothing the norm, or smart-casual for more upmarket establishments. Formality is more important when it comes to greetings, whether it be with friends, waiters, shop assistants, or hotel staff. Friends greet each other with a peck on the cheek.

F

Festivals

January

Orange Bowl. The final game between Florida's two best college football teams. Tel: 305-341-4700. New Year's Day.

Art Deco Weekend. A celebration of Miami Beach's famous Art Deco architecture. Events include a street fair, music, and an art show. Mid-January. Tel: 305-672-2014. www.artdecoweekend.com.

Dr Martin Luther King Jnr Day Parade. January 15th sees parades and celebrations in honor of the civil rights leader.

Miami Marathon and Half-Marathon. Late January is usually when the city's biggest marathon and half-marathon races take place. www.themiamimarathon.com.

February

Coconut Grove Arts Festival. The largest arts festival in Florida. Mid-February. Tel: 305-447-0401. www.coconutgroveartsfest.com.

Miami International Boat Show takes place mid-February over several days in Key Biscayne. www.miamiboatshow.com.

South Beach Wine and Food Festival. Huge festival runs for six days in late February. http://sobefest.com.

March

Carnaval Miami. Hispanic heritage festival in Little Havana usually starts in February and runs on into March. Tel: 305-644-8888. www.carnavalmiami.com.

Miami Open. This tennis tournament takes place in late March/early April at the Tennis Center at Crandon Park in Key Biscayne. www.miamiopen.com.

April

Miami Beach Gay Pride celebrations take place over three days in early April. www.miamibeachgaypride.com.

May

Miami Fashion Week. Showcase fashion event at the Convention Center. http://miamifashionweek.com.

October

Miami Broward Carnival. Day-long celebration of Caribbean culture in early October at the Miami–Dade County Fairgrounds. http://miamibrowardcarnival.com.

November

Miami International Auto Show. The city's big car show fills the Convention Center for ten days. www.sfliautoshow.com.

Miami Book Fair International. This international congress of authors, pub-

Sunset in Key West

lishers, and agents fills the city. Also street vendors, entertainment. Third week in November. Tel: 305-237-3258. www.miamibookfair.com.

December
Orange Bowl Parade. The nation's top marching bands accompany amazing floats before the football bowl game. December 31. Tel: 305-341-4700.

Gay and Lesbian Travelers

Although Florida as a whole is rather conservative, that's not the case everywhere and Miami, especially South Beach in particular, is very gay-friendly. For more information, contact the South Beach Business Guild (tel: 305-534-3336). The Gay and Lesbian Yellow Pages (tel: 800-697-2812; www.glyp.com) offers regional information on GLBT activities in Florida. The Damron Company (tel: 415-255-0404 or 800-462-6654; www.damron.com) publishes guides aimed at lesbians and gay men and lists gay-owned and gay-friendly accommodations nationwide.

Health

Most visitors to Miami will encounter no health problems during their stay: sunburn and mosquito bites in summer are the main nuisance. If you need medical assistance, ask the reception staff at your hotel or consult the Yellow Pages for the physician or pharmacist nearest. The larger resorts may have a resident doctor. If you need immediate attention, go to a hospital emergency room (ER).

Pharmacies and Hospitals
You'll find numerous CVS pharmacies and several Walgreens pharmacies in Miami, as well as independent pharmacies and some other pharmacy chains. You'll generally find good and helpful service. Many of these are open 24 hours, including the University Miami Hospital Pharmacy, 1400 NW 12th Avenue, Miami, FL 33136 (tel: 305-325-5722). This is also one of the city's major hospitals.

Insurance
There is nothing cheap about being sick in the US – whether it involves a simple visit to the doctor or a spell in a hospital. The initial fee charged by a good hospital might be $250, and that's before the additional cost of x-rays, medicines, examinations, and treatments have been added. Walk-in medical clinics are much cheaper than hospital emergency rooms for minor ailments. Foreign visitors are strongly advised to purchase travel insurance before leaving to avoid high urgent-care costs. Be sure you're covered for accidental death, emergency medical care, trip cancelation, and baggage or document loss.

On the beach at Key Largo

Health Hazards

Insects

People aren't the only creatures attracted to Florida's sun and sand. Miami sees its fair share of cockroaches, or palmetto bugs, fire ants, 'love bugs' (bibinoid flies), mosquitoes, and sand flies.

Sunburn

One of the most common sights in Florida is that of the over-baked tourist. If you are determined to get a suntan, do so gradually. Always wear a broad-brimmed hat, good-quality sunglasses, and use a high-factor sunscreen (40 plus) to protect your skin. Even on overcast days the sun's ultraviolet rays penetrate the clouds, giving you a false sense of safety. Dehydration and salt deficiency can lead to heat exhaustion, especially if taking medications or drinking alcohol or strong coffee. It's important to moderate these, drink plenty of water, and take time to acclimate to the heat and humidity if you aren't accustomed to it.

Heatstroke is a common problem for those from northern climates and is a potentially serious condition, so don't ignore the telltale signs. Long, uninterrupted periods of exposure to high temperatures can lead to heatstroke. If you feel dizzy and fuzzy-brained, feel muscle weakness and start to stumble, and your skin has become pale and dry rather than red and sweaty, immediately begin spraying yourself with water or, better yet, pour it on. To head off problems, keep major arteries in your neck cool by wearing a wet bandanna or cotton shirt with a collar.

Hours and Holidays

Stores are often open seven days a week and tend to stay open into the evening, especially in tourist areas. Government offices are usually open only on weekdays from 8am or 9am to 4pm or 5pm. Post offices are usually open weekdays from 8am to 5pm and have limited hours on Saturday morning.

Public holidays in the US include: New Year's Day (January 1), Martin Luther King's Birthday (January 15), President's Day (third Monday in February), Memorial Day (last Monday in May), Independence Day (July 4), Labor Day (first Monday in September), Columbus Day (second Monday in October), Veteran's Day (November 11), Thanksgiving (fourth Thursday in November), and Christmas Day (December 25).

Internet Facilities

The vast majority of accommodations in Miami will have WiFi available. The more expensive the property, the more likely you will have to pay for internet access, with more budget and mid-range accommodations offering free internet. Other options include using places like Starbucks and McDonald's, which offer free WiFi to customers, as do many bars.

Surf shop in Virginia Key

M

Media

The most widely read newspaper in Florida is the *Miami Herald*, which also has a very popular Spanish-language section sister paper, *El Nuevo Heraldo*. You can usually pick up *USA Today* from newspaper dispensers in the street or receive a free copy at certain hotel chains. Other national newspapers available in dispensers or good newsstands and bookstores include the *New York Times*, *Washington Post*, and *Wall Street Journal*. International newspapers are less common but can be found in some libraries, book stores, and cafés.

Money

American dollars come in bills of $1, $5, $10, $20, $50, and $100, all the same size. The dollar is divided into 100 cents. Coins come in 1 cent (penny), 5 cents (nickel), 10 cents (dime), 25 cents (quarter), 50 cents (half-dollar), and (rarely seen) $1 denominations.

Credit cards

All credit cards are widely accepted.

Cash machines

Cash or ATM machines are numerous throughout Miami.

Travelers' cheques

You can change travelers' cheques widely, and it will be easier if you get them in US dollars than in your own local currency.

Tipping

The US has a tipping culture and 15 percent is the norm for most things, sometimes 20 percent for especially good service. Have lots of $1 bills handy for tipping bellboys ($1 per bag), doormen, and anyone else who provides a service. Miami is notorious for adding tips to bills automatically, so always check to avoid double-tipping.

Taxes

Sales tax will be automatically added to your bills, and in Miami this is 7 percent. Of this, 1 percent is the county sales tax and 6 percent the Florida state sales tax. If you travel out of Miami–Dade County, the county tax rate may change.

P

Post

The US mail is run by the United States Postal Service (USPS), and private delivery services such as UPS and Fedex are usually used for bulkier, more valuable or more urgent items. Americans commonly complain about the USPS but the service is pretty reliable. You have to allow a few days if mailing items across the US. You can also buy stamps in some drugstores and hotels.

US mailboxes are blue and usually freestanding on the streets, though they are not as common as in European

St. Bernard de Clairvaux cloister

countries. Finding a post office is usually the best option. One of the main offices Downtown is at 150 SE 2nd Ave #103, Miami, FL 33131 (tel: 800 275-8777).

R

Religion

The US is predominantly a Christian country, and while most people are tolerant of other religions there are always exceptions, especially in the south.

S

Smoking

In Florida smoking is not allowed in bars, restaurants and other public places, although there are some exceptions so ask. As a rule, smoking is the exception rather than the norm.

T

Telephones

The area code for Miami is either 305 or 786. If dialling from overseas you must dial the full area code followed by the local number. If dialling from within the area code itself, you should still dial the full number with the area code.

The US country code is 1. To call the USA from Europe dial 00 followed by the country code, 1, followed by the area code and number. From Australia dial 0011 then the country code and number. If calling from Canada simply dial the country code, 1, followed by the number.

Mobile (Cell) Phones

In the US they are cell phones, not mobile phones. American cell phones use GSM 1900 or CDMA 800, a different frequency from other countries. Only foreign phones operating on GSM 1900 will work in the US. You may be able to take the SIM card from your home phone, install it in a rented cell phone in the US, and use it as if it's your own cell phone. Check with your own phone service provider before leaving. You could also consider buying a budget phone after you've arrived in the US, from somewhere like Walmart. TracFone and Net10 are popular, cheap non-contract options.

Cell phones can be rented for about $45–60 a week in the US. Also available are GSM 1900 compatible phones with prepaid calling time, such as those offered by T-Mobile (www.t-mobile. com). Be aware that you probably won't be able to pick up a signal in remote rural areas, such as the Everglades and the Florida Keys. Check the coverage before starting out.

Time Zones

The continental US is divided into four time zones. From east to west, later to earlier, they are Eastern Standard Time, Central Standard Time, Mountain Standard Time, and Pacific Standard Time, each separated by one hour. Miami is on Eastern Standard Time (EST), five hours behind Greenwich Mean Time. On the first Sunday in April, Floridians set the

Taxi on Ocean Drive

clock ahead one hour in observation of daylight saving time. On the last Sunday in October, the clock is moved back one hour to return to standard time. When it's noon in Miami it's also noon in New York, and 5pm in London.

Toilets

Ask for the restroom, not the toilet. Free public toilets are rare in Miami so look for larger department stores. If using one in a bar, a café or a store it's polite to buy something too, though not usually essential.

Tourist Information

The main tourist information office for Miami is the Greater Miami Convention and Visitors Bureau, which is in the Convention Center at 701 Brickell Avenue, Suite 2700 (tel: 305-539-3000 or 800-933-8448; www.miamiandbeaches. com). You can also find information at the Miami Beach Chamber of Commerce, 1920 Meridian Avenue, Suite 1 (tel: 305-674-1300; www.miamibeach chamber.com and www.miamibeach. com). Another good source of information is the Art Deco Welcome Center, 1001 Ocean Drive, Miami Beach (tel: 305-531-3484; www.mdpl.org).

Transportation

Arrival by Air

Miami International Airport (tel: 305-876-7000; www.miami-airport.com) is the main international airport for southern Florida and is 8 miles (13km) northwest of Downtown Miami. There are three terminals: North, Central, and South. International arrivals come in at both North and South terminals, depending on the airline. The Central terminal is used more by smaller and budget airlines, and there are plans to redevelop this in the next few years.

Miami is a major international arrival center for people transferring to other destinations, such as the Caribbean, for cruise ships, and for elsewhere in the US. Even if your final destination is Miami, you must be prepared for long waits at immigration.

Car Rental

If you're picking up a car when you arrive, all the major car rental companies have a presence at the airport, in the Car Rental Center at the airport's Central Station. See also 'Driving' below.

Taxis

A taxi from the airport to Downtown Miami should cost about $35–45. You'll find official taxi stands outside the baggage claim area.

Ground Transportation

The airport has good ground transportation connections into the city from the Central Station, which is connected to the airport by the MIA Mover electric train system, a fast and efficient way of moving people around the airport. At Central Station there are both Metrobus and Metrorail connections into the city. Tickets currently cost $2.25. There are also Hotel Shuttle and SuperShuttle services. You'll find stands outside the bag-

gage claim area. Beware of illegal touts for taxis and other services. The official systems work fine and are inexpensive.

Public Transportation

Miami has a good Metrobus and Metrorail public transportation system (www.miamidade.gov/transit), with a basic fare of $2.25 per ride. This allows for transfers and lasts for up to three hours. You can also get a 1-day pass for $5.65 and a 7-day pass for $29.25.

If using the Metrobus you can pay the flat fare in cash when you board, but you must have the right change and you forfeit the ability to transfer between buses. Metrorail does not accept cash fares. To use the system you must either have an EASYCard or an EASY ticket, which are also valid on Metrobus.

Miami also has a bike sharing scheme, with about 1,000 bikes available across 100 rental stations around the city. For details of how the scheme works visit http://citibikemiami.com.

EASY Cards and Tickets

The EASY Card is aimed more at residents though visitors can buy one too. You can get them at any Metrorail station, at ticketing kiosks throughout the city, at the airport, and at various stores and other outlets from pharmacies to liquor stores (www.miamidade.gov/transit/easy-card-sales-outlets.asp).

The card is a plastic credit-card style card which is valid for 20 years and can carry either a running balance you can top up, or a 1-day, 7-day or monthly travel pass. The basic card costs $2. You can buy and top it up online (https://transitstore.miamidade.gov/extern/products), and if you live in the US you can have it shipped to you before you travel to Miami.

The EASY Ticket can be more convenient for visitors. It works in much the same way as an EASY Card but is made of paper and lasts for only 60 days. If you're planning to use public transportation at least a few times, paying for an EASY Card is the best option.

Taxis

Miami taxis are yellow cabs. It can be hard to hail one on the streets so it's usually best to book one by phone or go to a taxi rank. The basic rate is currently $2.95 for the first 1/6 mile, and then $0.85 per 1/6 mile up to one mile. This makes the fare for a mile-long journey $7.20. After that the rate is $0.40 for each 1/6 mile, so a 2-mile trip would cost $9.60.

Local firms include American Taxi (305-947-3333), Miami–Dade Taxi (305-551-1111), Crown Taxi (305-445-5555) and Super Yellow Cab (305-888-7777).

Driving

Renting a car, and the price of gas, is cheaper in the US than in many countries so you might want to consider hiring a car for at least part of your vacation. It would allow you to do things like drive through the Florida Keys (see page 84) or explore more of the Everglades

(see page 79). However, if your main aim is to stay in Miami and enjoy it, you won't need a car. It's a busy city and traffic gets very congested, so a combination of walking, public transportation, and taxis should get you most places.

If you're visiting from elsewhere in the US and bringing your own car, allow for the traffic congestion when figuring out how long it will take to get from A to B. Miami is a long way from being as bad as Los Angeles, but it can still be very slow.

See also the Crime and Safety section for problems of relevance to motorists.

Driving on the Right
In the US they drive on the right. Visitors from countries like the UK, who drive on the left, should find it easy to adjust, especially as most US rental cars are automatics, giving you one less thing to think about.

Turning Right on a Red Light
When you come to a red light in Florida you must come to a complete stop. If you are in the right-hand lane you can then turn right on a red light if it is safe to do so and provided there isn't a NO TURN ON RED warning sign.

Priority to the Left
The US has very few roundabouts compared to other countries, although more are being introduced in parts of Florida. If approaching a roundabout then priority goes to traffic on your left. As many American drivers are not used to roundabouts, always be cautious when using one as not everyone is familiar with the rules.

If approaching a 2-way, 3-way or 4-way stop with other drivers coming, then priority goes to the first driver to reach the junction and stop. If one or more arrive at the same time, priority goes to the driver to your left. If priority is unclear then you just have to work it out.

Renting a Car
You must be 21 to rent a car in Florida, although if you're under 25 some companies may charge a higher rate. You will also need your passport, US or local driving license, and credit card. Without a credit card you will be expected to put down a hefty cash deposit. The major companies allow you to pick up in one location and drop off elsewhere, although sometimes this can incur a hefty fee.

Go over the insurance coverage provisions carefully with the agent before signing the rental agreement. Loss Damage Waiver (LDW), or Collision Damage Waiver (CDW), is essential. Without it, you'll be liable for any damage done to your vehicle in the event of an accident, regardless of whether or not you are to blame. You are advised to pay for supplementary liability insurance on top of standard third-party insurance. Insurance and tax charges can add a lot to an otherwise inexpensive rental, so take it into account in your budgeting. Also, be sure to check your rental car carefully for existing damage, and make a careful note of any dents or dings before leaving the lot.

Drink-driving
If you're under-21 in Florida then there is a zero-tolerance approach to

Brickell high-rises and the Rickenbacker Causeway to Key Biscayne

drink-driving and you cannot drive with a Blood Alcohol Content of higher than .02, which is the equivalent of one very small drink. If you're 21 or over then the limit is .08. This is not the equivalent of four drinks. There are heavy fines, the confiscation of your licence, and possibly even jail, so don't take the risk.

Car Hire Companies

All the major international car rental companies have offices both in Miami and at the airport. Some of the main names include Alamo (1-800-327-9633 or 305-633-6076), Avis (1-800-331-1212 or 305-341-0936), Budget (1-800-527-0700 or 305-871-2722), Enterprise (1-800-325-8007 or 305-633-0377), and Hertz (1-800-654-3131 or 305-871-0300).

Parking

Street parking at meters is hard to find and expensive, and a better option is to use a parking garage. There are numerous parking garages in Downtown Miami, and around, and competition keeps prices relatively low. For detailed information go to the website of the Miami Parking Authority: www.miamiparking.com.

Visas and Passports

Foreign travelers to the US (including those from Canada and Mexico) must carry a passport, valid for at least six months. A visa is required for visits of more than 90 days. A visa is also required by citizens of any countries not accepted in the US's Visa Waiver Program scheme, and for visits of over 90 days. Travelers from the UK, Australia, and New Zealand are all eligible for the Visa Waiver Program, but not those from Canada, who only require a passport. If eligible, the requisite details must be given when booking your ticket or before you travel otherwise you may be denied entry.

A return ticket is also normally required, and you may be asked to show it at immigration control. Note that if you have a connecting flight when traveling to the US, your point of entry is where you first touch down and you will be required to pass through immigration here. Immigration queues can be long and slow, so even if you have all the correct documentation, allow plenty of time to catch your connecting flight.

For the most current information, contact the US Department of Homeland Security at www.dhs.gov.

Weights and Measures

Miami, like the rest of the US, uses the Imperial system for weights and measures.

Women Travelers

Women travelers will be as safe in Miami as in any other large US city, with the usual proviso of avoiding unsafe areas (see also Crime and Safety).

Al Pacino in Scarface

BOOKS AND FILM

With its almost-guaranteed blue skies and sunshine by day, and colorful neon-lit nights, little wonder that Miami has appealed to movie- and TV-makers for so many years now. It forms a brilliant backdrop, particularly for stories of sleaze and crime. Crime writers such as Carl Hiaasen, Charles Willeford, and Janet Evanovich all feature the city alongside their casts of criminals, police, and private eyes.

In recent years younger writers – Cuban-Americans mostly – have started to tell the stories of people other than crooks and criminals.

The crooks and the cops who chase them do make for great stories, though. Mix in Miami's appeal to gangsters like Al Capone, stars like Frank Sinatra, and the crime and drug cartels from Russia, Colombia and especially Cuba, and you have a heady setting. One show in particular, *Miami Vice*, put the city onto TV screens around the world. It starred Don Johnson as the no-socks, t-shirt, linen suit-wearing Detective James 'Sonny' Crockett and Philip Michael Thomas as his equally suave partner Ricardo 'Rico' Tubbs, and although it only ran from 1984–89, it sure put Miami cool in the spotlight.

Books

Non-Fiction
Black Miami in the Twentieth Century by Marvin Dunn. The African-American side of this multi-faceted city, often overshadowed by the Hispanic culture.

Cuban Miami by Robert M Levine. The Cuban story told in a mix of essays, photographs, and cartoons.

Gangsters of Miami by Ron Chepesiuk. The lowdown on Al Capone, Myer Lansky, the Cuban Mafia, Russian Mafia and everyone else for who Miami is crime central.

Learning to Die in Miami by Carlos Eire. The author of the acclaimed *Waiting for Snow in Havana* recounts growing up in Miami.

Miami Then and Now by Carolyn Klepser and Arva Moore Parks. A look at the historical and contemporary development of Florida's famous city.

Miami by Joan Didion. Master journalist paints an in-depth portrait of the city.

Miami at Night by Bill Brothers. Photographic storytelling of Miami at its most exciting.

Miami Babylon: Crime, Wealth and Power by Gerald Posner. The underbelly of the city, the crime, the drugs, the political scandals.

Miami Architecture by Allan T. Shulman and Randall C. Robinson Jr. Good background reading on why Miami's buildings are so special.

Fiction
Darkly Dreaming Dexter by Jeff Lindsay. Miami murder and mayhem from criminal hero Dexter, later brought to TV.

Colin Farrell and Jamie Foxx in Miami Vice – the movie

Make Your Home Among Strangers by Jennine Capó Crucet. Award-winning debut novel by one of the new generation of Cuban-American writers in Miami.

Metro Girl by Janet Evanovich. Creator of the Stephanie Plum series, bestseller Evanovich creates a new heroine in Miami Beach, Alexandra Barnaby.

Miami Blues by Charles Willeford. Award-winning crime writer Willeford launches his Detective Hoke Moseley series in Miami.

Murder in Miami (The Cuban Trilogy) by Noel Hynd. Crime triology on Miami, Havana, and their drugs cartel links.

Rum Punch by Elmore Leonard. Partly set in Miami, this novel by crime maestro Leonard was filmed as *Jackie Brown* by Quentin Tarantino.

Tourist Season by Carl Hiaasen. One of numerous crime/comic novels set in Miami by *Miami Herald* journalist Hiaasen, this one involving corpses, crocodiles, politicians, and tourists.

Vagabond by Oscar Fuentes. Known as the Biscayne Poet, it's worth reading any of Oscar Fuentes' Miami-set collections of poetry, prose, and drama.

Film

Notorious (1946) Alfred Hitchcock's spy drama starring Cary Grant, Ingrid Bergman, and Claude Rains. Miami features in back-projection footage while the actors remained in Hollywood.

Goldfinger (1964) Ian Fleming's original Bond novel was partly set in Miami Beach and the movie featuring Sean Connery as 007 was also filmed there.

Thunderball (1965) Miami Beach is threatened with destruction in this Bond movie, with Sean Connery as 007 again, trying to prevent villain Emilio Largo and SPECTRE from achieving their evil aims.

Body Heat (1981) The dark and erotic thriller starring Kathleen Turner and William Hurt was set during a suitably steamy Florida summer. It was filmed in various places around Palm Beach County, part of the Greater Miami Metropolitan Area.

Scarface (1983) Brian de Palma's crime drama stars Al Pacino as a Cuban refugee who reaches Miami and rises to the top of the Cuban drug business there.

There's Something about Mary (1988) Directed by the Farrelly brothers, this quirky rom-com stars Cameron Diaz, Ben Stiller, and Matt Dillon and was filmed in Miami.

Miami Blues (1990) Alec Baldwin and Jennifer Jason Leigh were among the stars of this movie adaptation of Charles Willeford's crime novel and stayed true to the Miami location.

The Birdcage (1998) Directed by Mike Nichols, this remake of the 1978 comedy *La Cage aux Folles* was relocated to South Beach and starred Robin Williams and Gene Hackman.

Meet the Fockers (2004) The follow-up to *Meet the Parents* sees Jack Byrnes (Robert de Niro) driving his family to Miami for a memorably hilarious encounter with the Fockers, played by Dustin Hoffman and Barbra Streisand.

Miami Vice (2006) This remake of the hit TV series stars Jamie Foxx and Colin Farrell as detectives Tubbs and Crockett.

ABOUT THIS BOOK

This *Explore Guide* has been produced by the editors of Insight Guides, whose books have set the standard for visual travel guides since 1970. With top-quality photography and authoritative recommendations, these guidebooks bring you the very best routes and itineraries in the world's most exciting destinations.

BEST ROUTES

The routes in the book provide something to suit all budgets, tastes and trip lengths. As well as covering the destination's many classic attractions, the itineraries track lesser-known sights, and there are also excursions for those who want to extend their visit outside the city. The routes embrace a range of interests, so whether you are an art fan, a gourmet, a history buff or have kids to entertain, you will find an option to suit.

We recommend reading the whole of a route before setting out. This should help you to familiarise yourself with it and enable you to plan where to stop for refreshments – options are shown in the 'Food and Drink' box at the end of each tour.

For our pick of the tours by theme, consult Recommended Routes for… (see pages 6–7).

INTRODUCTION

The routes are set in context by this introductory section, giving an overview of the destination to set the scene, plus background information on food and drink, shopping and more, while a succinct history timeline highlights the key events over the centuries.

DIRECTORY

Also supporting the routes is a Directory chapter, with a clearly organised A–Z of practical information, our pick of where to stay while you are there and select restaurant listings; these eateries complement the more low-key cafés and restaurants that feature within the routes and are intended to offer a wider choice for evening dining. Also included here are some nightlife listings and our recommendations for books and films about the destination.

ABOUT THE AUTHORS

Mike Gerrard is a British travel writer who spends half the year at his home in Arizona, from where he travels widely in the US. He loves Florida, from its natural beauty and its wildlife to the fun of its theme parks and the buzz of cities like Miami, Orlando, and Tampa. He also updated *Insight Guide Florida*.

CONTACT THE EDITORS

We hope you find this Explore Guide useful, interesting and a pleasure to read. If you have any questions or feedback on the text, pictures or maps, please do let us know. If you have noticed any errors or outdated facts, or have suggestions for places to include on the routes, we would be delighted to hear from you. Please drop us an email at hello@insightguides.com. Thanks!

CREDITS

Explore Miami
Editor: Carine Tracanelli
Author: Mike Gerrard
Head of Production: Rebeka Davies
Update Production: Apa Digital
Picture Editor: Tom Smyth
Cartography: Carte
Photo credits: 4Corners Images 4/5T, 20, 28/29T; Alamy 16/17, 19, 50, 51, 78, 79, 83L; AWL Images 8/9T, 37; Bass 2 Billfish 24B; Courtesy of the Greater Miami Convention and Visitors Bureau, MiamiandBeaches. com 4MR, 21B, 24T, 43, 47, 49L, 48/49, 52, 55, 56/57, 76, 77L, 76/77; Daniel Azoulay/ Pérez Art Museum Miami 64/65; Fontaineb-leau 92; Frank Connor/Universal/Kobal/ REX/Shutterstock 121; Getty Images 6TL, 26, 27, 34, 36, 38, 40/41, 42, 53, 60, 61, 62, 64, 104; Hyatt 4MC, 8MC; iStock 4ML, 4ML, 6MC, 7MR, 8ML, 11, 12, 13B, 14B, 14T, 15L, 14/15, 16, 17L, 18, 28ML, 28MC, 28MR, 28ML, 28MC, 28MR, 30, 32, 33L, 39, 56, 57L, 59, 72/73, 74/75, 80, 81L, 80/81, 82, 82/83, 85L, 84/85, 86/87, 88, 108, 111, 112, 113, 116, 117; James Branaman/ Visit Florida 6ML; Leonardo 35, 90ML, 90MR, 90MR, 90MC, 90ML, 90/91T, 93, 96, 97, 102, 103; Leslie Joy Ickowitz/Visit Florida 21T, 68/69; Mandarin Oriental 90MC, 95, 101; Norbert Eisele-Hein/imageBRO/REX/ Shutterstock 70; Patrick Farrell/Visit Florida 8MC; Patrick Farrell/Visit Florida 7M, 8MR, 23L, 22/23, 48, 65L, 105, 106, 107; Peter W. Cross/Visit Florida 4MC, 7T, 8MR, 25, 44B, 45L, 68; Quarzo Hotel Bal Harbour 94; Scott Audette/Visit Florida 100; Shutterstock 1, 4MR, 6BC, 7MR, 10/11, 13T, 22, 31, 40, 41L, 44T, 44/45, 46, 58, 66, 67, 69L, 71, 84, 89L, 88/89, 109, 110, 114, 115, 118/119; Stephen Kubiak/Visit Florida 8ML; SuperStock 54, 63; Tap Tap 99; The Tides South Beach 32/33; Universal/Kobal/REX/ Shutterstock 120; Visit Florida 98
Cover credits: Getty Images (main) Shutter-stock (bottom)

Printed by CTPS – China

DISTRIBUTION

UK, Ireland and Europe
Apa Publications (UK) Ltd
sales@insightguides.com
United States and Canada
Ingram Publisher Services
ips@ingramcontent.com
Australia and New Zealand
Woodslane
info@woodslane.com.au
Southeast Asia
Apa Publications (Singapore) Pte
singaporeoffice@insightguides.com
Hong Kong, Taiwan and China
Apa Publications (HK) Ltd
hongkongoffice@insightguides.com
Worldwide
Apa Publications (UK) Ltd
sales@insightguides.com

SPECIAL SALES, CONTENT LICENSING AND COPUBLISHING

Insight Guides can be purchased in bulk quantities at discounted prices. We can create special editions, personalised jackets and corporate imprints tailored to your needs.
sales@insightguides.com
www.insightguides.biz

INDEX

MAP LEGEND

● Start of tour	▬▬ Railway	🎭 Theatre	
— Tour & route direction	▬▬ Motorway	✚ Church	
❶ Recommended sight	🚌 Main bus station	Lighthouse	
❷ Recommended restaurant/café	Ⓜ Metrorail station	Beach	
★ Place of interest	—●— Metromover station	Important building	
❶ Tourist information	✉ Main post office	Park	
✈ Airport	🗿 Statue/monument	Urban area	
	Ⓜ Museum/gallery	Non-urban area	

INSIGHT ⊙ GUIDES
OFF THE SHELF

Since 1970, INSIGHT GUIDES has provided a unique perspective on the world's best travel destinations by using specially commissioned photography and illuminating text written by local authors.

Whether you're planning a city break, a walking tour or the journey of a lifetime, our superb range of guidebooks and phrasebooks will inspire you to discover more about your chosen destination.

INSIGHT GUIDES
offer a unique combination of stunning photos, absorbing narrative and detailed maps, providing all the inspiration and information you need.

PHRASEBOOKS & DICTIONARIES
help users to feel at home, when away. Pocket-sized with a free app to download, they go where you do.

CITY GUIDES
pack hundreds of great photos into a smaller format with detailed practical information, so you can navigate the world's top cities with confidence.

EXPLORE GUIDES
feature easy-to-follow walks and itineraries in the world's most exciting destinations, with our choice of the best places to eat and drink along the way.

POCKET GUIDES
combine concise information on where to go and what to do in a handy compact format, ideal on the ground. Includes a full-colour, fold-out map.

EXPERIENCE GUIDES
feature offbeat perspectives and secret gems for experienced travellers, with a collection of over 100 ideas for a memorable stay in a city.